© iStockphoto.com

Enrichment Magazine

IN THIS ISSUE . . .

To the Director

This student folder contains nine study leaflets and the enrichment magazine. Remove the center staple and distribute the leaflets as indicated in the leaders guide. This magazine should be distributed at the first session for use throughout the course.

3558 S. Jefferson Ave., St. Louis, MO 63118-3968

1-800-325-3040 • www.cph.org

Written by Reed Lessing

Edited by Brian Chisamore

Cover illustration © CPH/Gerad Taylor

This publication may be available in braille, in large print, or on cassette tape for the visually impaired. Please allow 8 to 12 weeks for delivery. Write to Lutheran Blind Mission, 7550 Watson Rd., St. Louis, MO 63119-4409; call toll-free 1-888-215-2455; or visit the Web site: www.blindmission.org.

Manufactured in the United States of America

1 2 3 4 5 6 7 8 9 10 21 20 19 18 17 16 15 14 13 12

Learning to Love Leviticus

Leviticus used to be the first book Jewish children studied in the synagogue. In the modern Church, it tends to be the last part of the Scriptures anyone cares to look at. For some, Leviticus is the "liver and onions" book of the Bible. It must be good for us, but we just don't seem to have a taste for the stuff. For others, Leviticus is something like exercise. They tried it once, and that was enough to last a lifetime.

So, what is your problem with Leviticus? Maybe you think it is too legalistic. Why, with all its "thou shalts" and "thou shalt nots," especially related to a worship system so foreign to us, perhaps the book is too formal and ceremonial for you. Leviticus is also full of blood. Chapter after chapter, in great detail, animals are sliced and severed and then sacrificed. There are also parts of the book that seem like they come from another planet; things like Urim and Thummim (8:8), unauthorized fire (10:1), and eruptions of the skin (13:2).

Wouldn't it be easier to speed-read our way through Leviticus and get on to something more relevant and applicable? Before we do that, however, let's consider these words from Paul, "For *whatever* was written in former days was written for our instruction, that through endurance and through the encouragement of the Scriptures we might have hope" (Romans 15:4, emphasis added). So Leviticus is not only for Israel's instruction, but also for *ours*? And the apostle maintains that the book will encourage us and fill us with *hope*? Jesus goes so far as to say that to understand His death and resurrection, we need to search the Pentateuch, and this, of course, includes Leviticus. In fact, New Testament writers quote from or refer to the Book of Leviticus at least forty times. All right then, let's learn to love Leviticus!

Such a Bloody Book

The book continues several of the major motifs from the Book of Exodus. For instance, in Exodus, God tells Moses the Israelites are a priestly nation, and Leviticus lays out many priestly regulations. In the Book of Exodus, the design for the tabernacle is given, while much of Leviticus explains how it is to function as a means of grace and, as such, is the tabernacle's users' manual. At the end of Exodus, the Lord's presence descends on the tabernacle. In Leviticus, the implications of His presence are spelled out.

The main link, though, between Exodus and Leviticus is blood. Moses mediates a covenant of blood (Exodus 24:1–8) and explains its significance throughout the Book of Leviticus. For instance, blood is sprinkled seven times before the Lord at the sanctuary, as well as on the front of the Mercy Seat. It is placed on the lobe of Aaron's right ear, on the thumb of his right hand, and on the big toe of his right foot. Why all the blood? Blood is shed to reconcile people with God. "Without the shedding of blood there is no forgiveness of sin" (Hebrews 9:22).

The massive amount of blood sprinkled throughout Leviticus prepares us to understand the ministry of the Suffering Servant, who sprinkles many nations with blood. The verb translated "sprinkle" appears twenty-four times in the Old Testament, with twenty of them coming in Leviticus and Numbers. A close synonym describes Moses' action of sprinkling Israel with the "blood of the covenant" (Exodus 24:8). Because Jesus is the Suffering Servant, New Testament writers employ the action of sprinkling to denote Christ's work as our great High Priest. His sprinkled blood earned for us complete forgiveness for all our sins. When John the Baptist sees Jesus, he proclaims, "Behold, the Lamb of God, who takes away the sin of the world!" (John 1:29). Jesus is the culmination and consummation of every blood sacrifice in the Book of Leviticus.

But Leviticus includes more than blood offerings. The grain offering is another prominent sacrifice. Though it was not a sacrifice of blood to atone for sins, the grain offering was still beneficial. Consider this statement: "You shall season all your grain offerings with salt. You shall not let the salt of the covenant with your God be missing from your grain offering; with all your offerings you shall offer salt" (Leviticus 2:13). Two other passages associate the Lord's covenants with salt. Within the context of establishing Aaron as the priestly family line, God promises to sustain them through Israel's offerings. This is a "covenant of salt forever before the LORD for you and for your offspring with you" (Numbers 18:19). Then, within the framework of the Davidic covenant, Abijah says, "Ought you not to know that the LORD God of Israel gave the kingship over Israel forever to David and his sons by a covenant of salt?" (2 Chronicles 13:5). "Forever" gives us insight into the use of salt in the grain offering. Salt, after all, does not burn. Neither does it turn into gas. Salt survives fire intact. Just as salt abides for a long time, so the Lord's covenant love endures forever. Paul puts it this way: "For I am sure that neither death nor life, nor angels nor rulers, nor things present nor things to come, nor powers, nor height nor depth, nor anything else in all creation, will be able to separate us from the love of God in Christ Jesus our Lord" (Romans 8:38–39).

Though blood and grain offerings are prominent in Leviticus, the book contains much more than just commands related to worship. God is also concerned with conduct outside of worship. For example, the familiar words "You shall love your neighbor as yourself" appear in Leviticus 19:18. Paul quotes this verse (Romans 13:9; Galatians 5:14). Then there is the command to be holy. The apostle Peter takes this up when he writes, "But as He who called you is holy, you also be holy in all your conduct, since it is written, 'You shall be holy, for I am holy'" (1 Peter 1:15–16). This comports with his teaching that the Body of Christ is a priestly nation.

Yes, Yes, a Thousand Times Yes

So, is Leviticus really the dour, depressing, peculiar book we so often make it out to be? Although at times it may seem that way, it really isn't. Yes, it is a book filled with many rituals that are foreign to us. But there is a reason for that. The rituals are foreign to us because they are no longer performed. They are no longer performed because they have been completely, absolutely, and eternally fulfilled.

They are fulfilled in Christ Jesus. Every promise in Leviticus is "yes" in Christ (2 Corinthians 1:20). This means we have a great High Priest who makes for us a new way into God's presence. In Christ, we have blood that cleanses our conscience (Hebrews 9:14) and a single sacrifice that forgives us once and for all. Overwhelmed by this love, Paul employs sacrificial ideas taken from the Book of Leviticus when he writes, "I appeal to you therefore, brothers, by the mercies of God, to present your bodies as a living sacrifice, holy and acceptable to God, which is your spiritual worship" (Romans 12:1). Indeed, the best way to love Leviticus is to love the Lord of Leviticus. We joyfully offer ourselves to Him because He first offered His life on the cross for us.

Holy, Holy, Holy

We often sing the lyrics to this hymn in church: "Holy, holy, holy! Lord God Almighty! Early in the morning our song shall rise to Thee" (*LSB* 507). But what does *holy* actually mean? We often associate the word with ideas such as being righteous, pious, perfect, and morally upright. But in Hebrew, *holy* denotes what is separate. To illustrate, the word first appears in the establishment of the Sabbath to distinguish this day from the previous six. Genesis 2:3 states, "So God blessed the seventh day and made it holy, because on it God rested from all His work that He had done in creation." From here on out, *holy* is the word of choice when Old Testament authors describe God. He is separate, distinct, and different from everything and everyone else in all creation. Even at that, because of His great mercy and love for us, the Lord yearns to be present in our lives.

The problem, though, is this. Unregulated contact with the Lord results in death, regardless of our motives. Uzzah, for example, is killed by God when he steadies the ark of the covenant (a holy object), regardless of his good intention (2 Samuel 6:6–11). How then is this holy God able to take up residency in our lives without destroying us?

Separate, Yet with Us Always

Israel's freedom from Egyptian slavery begins when the Lord comes to Moses in a burning bush. This place is holy ground. After Pharaoh's army drowns in the Red Sea, God meets his people at Mount Sinai. Israel is encamped below; the Lord is on the mountain's summit. The solution to this separation between God and His people is the construction of a sanctuary.

The Lord commands Moses, "And let them make Me a sanctuary, that I may dwell in their midst" (Exodus 25:8). The sanctuary brings heaven to earth, allowing God to be present with His people. After the sanctuary is built, the Lord descends the mountain and fills it. But then there is a problem. "Moses was not able to enter the tent of meeting because the cloud settled on it, and the glory of the Lord filled the tabernacle" (Exodus 40:35). The Book of Exodus ends with a huge dilemma. What good is God's presence in the sanctuary if the people are unable to have access to Him?

The solution to the problem is the ordination of priests. At the end of the Book of Exodus, God separates out a group, the priesthood, to work within the sanctuary and mediate His holy presence to Israel through sacred rites. The office of the high priest is described in Exodus 28–30, but the ordination rite does not take place until Leviticus 8–9.

The office of priest is grounded in the divine demand to wear holy clothes. God commands Moses, "And you shall make holy garments for Aaron your brother, for glory and for beauty" (Exodus 28:2). This focus on clothing underscores the central role of the priest to mediate God's presence through sacred rites. The vestments serve to protect the priest, much like firefighters wear gear to protect them from fire. The vestments also transform the priest so he is capable of bridging the gap between God and Israel.

But the vocation of the priesthood is not simply an instance of "the-clothes-makes-the-person." Priests, too, undergo a process of purification and become holy (Exodus 28; Leviticus 8). We may think of this separation as hierarchical and, as such, an instance of power and privilege.

However, when the office of priest is viewed as a license for personal promotion, it results in death to the priest. This is illustrated in the story of Aaron's two eldest sons, Nadab and Abihu (Leviticus 10:1–2). God kills them for offering unholy fire at the altar. The text is vague about their exact actions, but the rebuke of Moses to Aaron suggests that the two priests were viewing their office as one of privilege, rather than service. God's intention is for priests to lose their freedom for the sake of the larger community. Individual priests are called to give up their autonomy and become mediators of God's presence in the setting of the sanctuary.

To do so, priests offered the whole burnt offering, the sin offering, the guilt offering, and the peace offering. The transfer of God's blessing to Israel is another aspect of the mediating role of the priest. Aaron assumed this office when he blessed the camp from the door of the sanctuary (Leviticus 9:22–24; Numbers 6:21–26).

Jesus is our Great High Priest who finally and fully bridges the gap between people and God the Father. This is the main gist of the Epistle to the Hebrews. The author refers to various texts from the Old Testament (e.g., Psalm 110:1, 4; Leviticus 16; Jeremiah 31:31–34) in order to demonstrate that, through Christ, "A better hope is introduced, through which we draw near to God" (Hebrews 7:19).

Royal and Holy, Now and Forever

The priestly vocation of Jesus, however, does not eliminate the vocation of priests. The apostles are baptized with fire and commanded to preach the Word and administer the Sacraments. The Church will always need pastors who give up their freedom in order to mediate God's holy presence. Through the pastors' administration of the Means of Grace, all Christians are empowered to be a "royal priesthood" and a "holy nation" (1 Peter 2:9). We know that holiness is infiltrating our larger world when we follow in Christ's footsteps, announce to the world our hope in Christ, and patiently suffer for the Gospel. The priestly vocation of ordained pastors in the sanctuary and the priestly vocation of the laity in the world work in tandem to fulfill the divine mandate to make disciples of all nations. In this way, more and more people will unite with us when we joyfully sing, "Holy, holy, holy! Lord God Almighty!"

I Hate, I Despise Your Feasts

"I hate, I despise your feasts." Who would say this of Israel's worship? Maybe it was Pharaoh. Moses once asked him to let the Israelites travel three days into the wilderness to sacrifice to the Lord. Pharaoh mockingly responded, "Who is the LORD that I should obey His voice and let Israel go?" (Exodus 5:2). Or perhaps the person who derides and ridicules Israel's feasts is the Assyrian field commander who lived during the days of Hezekiah. He says, for example, "Do not let Hezekiah make you trust in the LORD by saying, 'The LORD will surely deliver us'" (Isaiah 36:15).

Truth be told, it was the *Lord God of Israel* who said, "I hate, I despise your feasts, and I take no delight in your solemn assemblies. Even though you offer Me your burnt offerings and grain offerings, I will not accept them; and the peace offerings of your fattened animals, I will not look upon them. Take away from Me the noise of your songs; to the melody of your harps I will not listen" (Amos 5:21–23). Shocking indeed! What is going on here?

Seemingly Perfect, Yet Fatally Flawed

The Books of Leviticus, Numbers, and Deuteronomy are chock-full of regulations for Israel's worship. There are prescriptions for burnt offerings (Leviticus 1), grain offerings (Leviticus 2), peace offerings (Leviticus 3), sin offerings (Leviticus 4), and guilt offerings (Leviticus 5:14–6:7). Festivals include the Day of Atonement (Leviticus 16), Ingathering (Exodus 23:16), Firstfruits (Leviticus 23:9–14), Unleavened Bread (Exodus 29:2), Booths (Leviticus 23:33–43), Passover (Exodus 12), and, of course, the weekly Sabbath observance. Why, then, does the Lord hate and despise these solemn rites?

Through Amos and other prophets, God rejects Israel's worship. The heart of the problem was a problem of the heart. "This people draw near with their mouth and honor Me with their lips, while their hearts are far from Me" (Isaiah 29:13). The attitude was "Anything goes as long as the rituals and sacrifices are done in good order."

Amos 4:4–5 is instructive. Imitating the call to worship, verse 4 begins with a command, "Come to Bethel." Then the other shoe drops. Instead of continuing with the theme of worship, kneeling or bowing down, he says, "and transgress," the same word the prophet uses throughout Amos 1:3–2:3 to describe "crimes against humanity." The bombshell in Amos 4:4 is that the same idea is used to describe Israel's worship life. Imagine this sign on a marquee outside your sanctuary, "Come to This Church and Sin!"

Amos 4:4–5 sounds more like a list that a church would draw up to describe their "member of the year," rather than an indictment for excommunication. After all, the people were attending worship services and going beyond the call of duty with their offerings and tithes. However, Israelites had the form of godliness but denied its power. Worship had been transformed into a fraudulent form of escape for the elite, who practiced social oppression and then flocked into the pews at every opportunity. Worship had become a barrier to true faith.

The second part of Amos 4:4 sheds more light on the problem. The prophet calls them "*your* sacrifices" and "*your* tithes." Israel's worship did not involve the Lord; if it did, Amos would have called them "*His* sacrifices" and "*His* tithes." People "love to do" their liturgical acts (Amos 4:5). Israel's sense of love, though, was not for the Lord and their neighbor (Deuteronomy 6:5; Leviticus 19:18). They only loved their religious rituals at their shrines. Israelites loved the sacrificial system more than they loved their poor and oppressed neighbors.

This is a far cry from this apostolic admonition: "Present your bodies as a living sacrifice" (Romans 12:1), with the ensuing exhortation to "associate with the lowly" (Romans 12:16). Israel made God's house into "a den of robbers" (Jeremiah 7:11; Luke 19:46). To be sure, there was nothing wrong with the sacrifices and offerings described in Amos 4:4–5 that made Israel transgress. These were God's gracious gifts. But in the context of Israel's blatant unrighteousness and impenitence, these sacrifices and offerings became a mockery and a sin.

The main issue, then, was not Israel's worship, but Israel's conduct *outside* of worship. Amos does not offer the people advice to make their festivals more meaningful. He does not suggest "a few less sacrifices here, a few more songs there." The only remedy is consistent moral and ethical action. If justice and righteousness are not present, worship with all its ritual accoutrements is a sham.

God's critiques in the Book of Amos against Israel's worship life appear to be a total about-face from Mosaic commands and ordinances in the Pentateuch. But this is not the case. God is no more against sacrifices than He is against psalms and songs (Amos 5:23). The same holds true in the Book of Isaiah. He also preached against Israel's new moon festivals, appointed feasts, and the like. However, he also included prayer in the same category. It is only when the sacrificial system and ceremonial laws became a *substitute* for morality and a life with the Lord that the prophets inveigh so heavily against them (cf. Isaiah 58:6–7). First John 3:18 states: "Little children, let us not love in word or talk but in deed and in truth." Sacrificial action was to empower sacrificial lives. They are designed to go together. God wants both sacrifices and a people willing to sacrifice for Him.

On the other hand, there are times when Old Testament prophets speak positively about Israel's worship life. Isaiah's call came when he was worshiping in the temple, and he affirms worship in the temple in, for example, Isaiah 44:28; 52:11; 66:20–24. Jeremiah and Ezekiel both follow suit. The post-exilic prophets Haggai and Zechariah advocate rebuilding the temple and stir up the people to reestablish their worship life.

Faith and Life

"I hate, I despise your feasts." God still says this when our worship disintegrates into simply going through the motions. This is a temptation for us just as it was for the ancient Israelites. It can be so easy for us, as we go about our daily lives, to largely forget our desperate spiritual need. Even though we may come to the Lord in prayer or worship, our motivation can be based more on habit than on faith. This is a real and frightening prospect. We should always remember that God is against outward rites that do not entail the inward sacrifice of a broken and contrite heart. The Means of Grace, received in worship, do not grant forgiveness apart from faith.

Through our faith in Christ—our trust and belief in the promises God has made to us and fulfilled for us in Jesus—we receive His full and unconditional forgiveness and acceptance. Through faith, forgiveness is received, and it is through that faith that prayers and worship have any value. As we come to God with trust and belief in Jesus, God is pleased with us—with our worship and our lives.

© Tammy Bryngelson/iStockphoto.com

Conquering **Complaining**

When was the last time you encountered someone who complained about everything under the sun? Did you purposely seek him out to have another conversation? Probably not. In all likelihood, you said to yourself, "I hope I don't have to talk to that person again!" We would rather talk with people who don't complain and, when faced with setbacks, look for solutions.

Does a positive and upbeat approach to life's obstacles describe you? What do you do when things go wrong? What do you say when you get hot and bothered? Do you accept it, deal with it, and move forward? Or do you throw a pity party?

As sons of Adam and daughters of Eve, there are times when everyone gives in to whimpering and whining. There are even occasions when we find ourselves complaining about the smallest of things. "I asked for extra ice in my tea!" "My shirts are folded with the crease up!" "How dare you track mud on my clean carpet!" Job's words become our motto: "I will give free utterance to my complaint; I will speak in the bitterness of my soul" (Job 10:1). Though venting can be helpful at times, perpetual grumbling about things damages our spirits and turns people off. If releasing all of our broken emotions was truly cathartic, complaining would rid us of the need to complain. Instead, however, it solidifies our stubbornness, hardens our hearts, and damages people in our lives. Soon, we are addicted to negativity. Let's face it. Complaining is costly, contagious, sometimes catastrophic, and always way too comfortable. Just ask Israel!

© iStockphoto.com

Poor, Poor, Pitiful Me

Life in the desert was difficult for God's people. The Hebrew term for desert (*midbar*) does not denote a place of blowing sand and occasional palm trees. Rather, *midbar* is a locale that does not provide enough resources to sustain people. The word comes 271 times in the Old Testament; 105 of them are in the Pentateuch. The events in the Book of Leviticus are set in the *midbar* of Sinai, but Numbers is the book that has the most to say about life in the wilderness. Its name in Hebrew is *bemidbar*, which means "in the wilderness."

The Lord guided His people through the barren wasteland with smoke and fire, His divine messenger, and the ark of the covenant. He provided water, food, and clothing. And what did Israel do most of the time in the wilderness? They "murmured in their tents" (Psalm 106:25). The nation had at least four kinds of complainers.

1. The martyr. These people interpret every setback as though it is the end. They are frequently known to say, "This is going to kill me!" Just after Israel left Egypt and *before* crossing the Red Sea, some complained, "It would have been better for us to serve the Egyptians than to die in the wilderness" (Exodus 14:12). When faced with a challenging situation, they immediately arrive at the worst-case scenario—death!

2. The whiner. This individual's litany is "It's not fair!" Moses takes the role of chief whiner when he asks the Lord, "Why have You dealt ill with Your servant? And why have I not found favor in Your sight, that You lay the burden of all this people on me?" (Numbers 11:11). Here is Israel's leader bellyaching that God is unjust!

3. The cynic. The mantra for these folks is "Nothing will ever change!" Some Israelites took up this dirge: "But now our strength is dried up, and there is nothing at all but this manna to look at" (Numbers 11:6). They are sick and tired of manna waffles, manna hotcakes, manna bagels, and manna soufflé. Things will *never* get better!

4. The perfectionist. These people love to ask, "Is that your *very* best?" They take the position of judge and jury and condemn us for not measuring up to their expectations. "But the people thirsted there for water, and the people grumbled against Moses and said, 'Why did you bring us up out of Egypt, to kill us and our children and our livestock with thirst?'" (Exodus 17:3).

What is God's response to all of this moaning and groaning? He sent fire, a plague, an earthquake, snakes, as well as forty years in the wilderness. The Lord takes a hard line against whimpering and whining! So what can we do?

Is There Really Reason to Complain?

1. Forget where I have been. This was difficult for Israel. "The rabble that was among them had a strong craving. And the people of Israel wept again and said, 'Oh that we had meat to eat! We remember the fish we ate in Egypt that cost nothing, the cucumbers, the melons, the leeks, the onions and the garlic'" (Numbers 11:4–5). Egypt never looked so good! Israelites even went so far as to refer to their place of bondage as "a land flowing with milk and honey" (Numbers 16:13). Becoming so transfixed on the past, we miss God's current work in our lives. Rather than looking back on the "glory days" and living with nostalgic angst, God wants us to make this confession: "I will say to the LORD, 'My refuge and my fortress, my God, in whom I trust'" (Psalm 91:2).

2. Don't become focused on where I am. When some Israelites returned from spying in the Promised Land, they said, "The land, through which we have gone to spy it out, is a land that devours its inhabitants, and all the people that we saw in it are of great height. And there we saw the Nephilim (the sons of Anak, who come from the Nephilim), and we seemed to ourselves like grasshoppers, and so we seemed to them" (Numbers 13:32–33). If in looking back we get stuck in reminiscing, then looking around at the current state of affairs gets us lost in our problems. They become huge, like giants, and we become small and powerless, like grasshoppers!

3. Concentrate on where I am going. Joshua and Caleb are men of faith. They focus on the future. These two faithful spies dare to say, "If the LORD delights in us, He will bring us into this land and give it to us, a land that flows with milk and honey" (Numbers 14:8). At His second coming, Jesus will appear in glory to usher us into the heavenly promised land. John says this about the New Jerusalem: "They will need no light of lamp or sun, for the Lord God will be their light, and they will reign forever and ever" (Revelation 22:5). The free gift of eternal life is ours because Jesus prevailed over the wilderness and all its temptations. Our Savior was further tested at the cross and overcame His enemies there as well. Because of His resurrection victory, we await "our blessed hope, the appearing of the glory of our great God and Savior Jesus Christ" (Titus 2:13). In this we rejoice.

What Could There Ever Be to Complain About?

Certainly our lives can be harsh, our circumstances can be difficult, and our futures can seem uncertain. There is always the temptation before us to complain that we are being mistreated or neglected by God. It can be so inviting for us to wallow in self-pity and wish that things were different.

But at times like that, what can we say but that we have forgotten a few things! God has been merciful to us at all times. He has sustained us in this life, that we may receive the blessings that our Lord Christ came into the world to achieve for us: forgiveness of sins and life everlasting. When we consider these tremendous gifts, we can only stop and wonder and ask, "What is there ever to complain about?"

Strike the Rock

© Rafal Dubiel/iStockphoto.com

Kids are camels! I realized this in new and profound ways when we had our three children: Abi Joy, Jonathan Curtis, and Lori Beth Lessing. These kids could—even on a hot Oklahoma summer day—play all morning, play all afternoon, and even play into the evening without ever needing a drink. "Are you thirsty yet?" "No way, Dad!" Miles and miles they would go. When offered water, they'd say, "No!"

Our three children were just fine until their angelic heads hit the pillow. Then it began. I can still hear our firstborn: "Daddy, I need a *dink*." "How cute," my wife and I would muse. Little Abi needs a "dink." It had a charming sound. Our daughter was amusing, pleasant, even entertaining—that is, until 8:00 p.m. became 9:00 p.m. and 9:00 p.m. turned into 9:45 p.m.

One night, feeling more like a mighty Hebrew prophet confronting a wayward Judean king than a caring shepherd of tender sheep, I blurted out, "Abi, the next time you ask for a drink, I'll spank you!" There, I thought, that should bring peace and quiet to the Western Front. A few minutes later, the golden silence was broken. I heard a voice crying in the wilderness, "Daddy, when you come and spank me, please bring me a *dink*!"

No Water in the Desert

Imagine *thousands* of discordant voices crying out to you, "There is no water to drink" (Numbers 20:5). Living in the eastern Nile Delta, Israelites had grown accustomed to water. Even when leaving Egypt, they have no problems with water. Do they need it to form into walls? No problem. Do they need it to come crashing down on Pharaoh's horses and chariots? Easy as pie! When confronted with bitter water just after the exodus, Moses throws a piece of wood into the putrid pool. Presto—instant purified water. So where is their source of fresh water now that they are encamped at Kadesh? Have no fear. Moses is here! He deserves the title "The Wonderful Wizard of Waterworks." As a child, Moses is placed into water for safety and drawn out of water for salvation (Exodus 2:1–9). His soon-to-be-bride Zipporah describes him with these words: "He even drew water for us and watered the flock" (Exodus 2:19). Then at Rephidim, he strikes the rock, and water comes out of it for Israelites to drink.

But at Kadesh, even Moses doesn't know what to do. He can only fall facedown before the Lord. The combination of heat and thirst causes cramps in people's legs, arms, and stomachs. Prolonged thirst also brings with it headaches, dizziness, mental confusion, excessive sweating, and moist, clammy skin.

These events at Kadesh took place halfway around the world and over three thousand years ago. What do they have to do with us?

Our Own Desert Places

Though we don't call it "Kadesh," we all have a place or two in our lives where we are burned out. Perhaps it is fear too deep to manage, loneliness too heavy to bear, or doubts too many to number. Kadesh is the place where our relationships are dehydrated, dry, and almost dead. Some have spotted Kadesh in homes, when spouses get upset, kids don't listen, and people wonder what on earth they should do with all the tension. And Kadesh is in every church. It's the place where, try as we might, everything looks dry as dust. Miles and miles we go. When offered water, we say, "No!" That is, until we acknowledge the depth of our thirst.

At our burned-out place, we cry, "As a deer pants for flowing streams, so pants my soul for You, O God. My soul thirsts for God, for the living God" (Psalm 42:1–2). We feel the anguish of these words: "O God, You are my God; earnestly I seek You; my soul thirsts for You; my flesh faints for You, as in a dry and weary land where there is no water" (Psalm 63:1).

How will our thirst ever be quenched? It will take a staff, but it can't be any ordinary, run-of-the-mill staff. It has to be *the* staff. You remember! The staff that goes back and forth from a stick to a snake. The staff that struck the mighty Nile and turned its water into blood. The staff that was stretched out over the Red Sea to divide its waters. God commanded Moses, "Take the staff, and assemble the congregation, you and Aaron your brother" (Numbers 20:8). Then Moses struck the rock with this staff. Water gushed out, and there was enough water for Israelites and their animals to drink.

Moses isn't the only person who knows about the power of a staff. So does Matthew. He writes about Jesus: "They put a staff in His right hand and knelt in front of Him and mocked Him. 'Hail, king of the Jews!' they said. They spit on Him, and took the staff and struck Him on the head again

© Jason Doiy/iStockphoto.com

and again" (Matthew 27:29–30 NIV). For Jesus, any ordinary, run-of-the-mill staff will do. Any stick that remotely looks like a king's scepter is just fine. Any piece of wood is bound to work, provided it won't break when slapped repeatedly against someone's head. And make sure that the stick can be carved to include a pointed, sharp end, because the Rock finally has to be split and opened up. John saw it happen. He writes, "But one of the soldiers pierced His side with a spear, and at once there came out blood and water" (John 19:34).

Water flowed from the One whose lips had been cracked and swollen. Water flooded from the One whose body had blistered and burned under the hot Palestinian sun. Water gushed out of the side from the One who could barely muster the energy to cry out, "I thirst" (John 19:28). Strike the rock, and water will come out of it for the people to drink. And they did. And it flowed. And we live!

God's Living Water

Old Testament prophets envision the day when we will be given living water. Isaiah sees a long-awaited summer rain: "The burning sand shall become a pool, the thirsty ground springs of water" (Isaiah 35:7). Ezekiel envisions a reservoir teaming with life: "Everything will live where the river goes" (Ezekiel 47:9). Joel sees an abundant oasis: "All the streambeds of Judah shall flow with water; and a fountain shall come forth from the house of the LORD" (Joel 3:18). Miles and miles we go. When offered this water, all too often we still say, "No!"

All that changes when we come to the Rock. Our Lord Christ Jesus is that Rock who was crushed for us, yet is alive forevermore. As the water flowed from the rock in the wilderness, Christ's forgiveness flows to us here in the barren wilderness of life in this fallen world. His forgiveness flows as water with the Word in the Sacrament of Holy Baptism. His forgiveness continues to wash over us throughout our lives as His Word is spoken to us. His forgiveness comes to us in His own true body and blood in the Supper He has given us. Such an abundant flood! Such a life-giving spring! From this Rock of Jesus Christ, indeed we are sustained and preserved, throughout this life and even forever.

© Tobias Helbig/iStockphoto.com

Study Guide

LifeLight

LifeLight Expands

Available NOW!

The Bible: An Overview
Genesis, Pt. 1
Genesis, Pt. 2
Exodus, Pt. 1
Exodus, Pt. 2
Wilderness Wanderings
Joshua
Judges
Ruth/Esther
1 & 2 Samuel
Life of David

Job
Selected Psalms
Proverbs
Ecclesiastes/Song of Solomon
Isaiah, Pt. 1
Isaiah, Pt. 2
Daniel
Minor Prophets
Matthew, Pt. 1
Matthew, Pt. 2

Mark
Luke, Pt. 1
Luke, Pt. 2
John, Pt. 1
John, Pt. 2
Acts, Pt. 1
Acts, Pt. 2
Romans, Pt. 1
Romans, Pt. 2
1 Corinthians
2 Corinthians

Galatians/Philippians/Colossians
Ephesians/1 & 2 Thessalonians
Timothy/Titus/Philemon
Hebrews
James/Jude
1 & 2 Peter
1, 2, 3 John
Revelation

LifeLight Foundations

Baptism
Bible Feasts
Creation, New Creation

The Christian's Mission
Law & Gospel
Ministry

Miracles
Prayer
Prophecy

Triune God
Worship

LifeLight Release Schedule

2012 RELEASES

LifeLight Foundations—Heaven & Hell	October

2013 RELEASES

LifeLight—Ezra/Nehemiah	January
LifeLight—1 & 2 Kings	April
LifeLight—Haggai/Zechariah/Malachi	July
LifeLight Foundations—Parables	October

2014 RELEASES

LifeLight—Nahum/Habakkuk/Zephaniah	January
LifeLight—1 & 2 Chronicles	April
LifeLight—Hosea/Joel/Amos	July
LifeLight Foundations—End Times	October

How Did We Get Here?

Distribute before session 1 for use in session 1.
Use enrichment magazine pp. 2–7.

Exodus; Numbers 7–9; 11; 13–14; Deuteronomy 5–8

Resources for Worship

Use these resources for your daily study at home and at the week's assembly.

Hymn

Guide me, O Thou great Redeemer,
Pilgrim through this barren land.
I am weak, but Thou art mighty;
Hold me with Thy pow'rful hand.
Bread of heaven, bread of heaven,
Feed me till I want no more;
Feed me till I want no more.

Open now the crystal fountain
Whence the healing stream doth flow;
Let the fiery, cloudy pillar
Lead me all my journey through.
Strong deliv'rer, strong deliv'rer,
Be Thou still my strength and shield;
Be Thou still my strength and shield.

When I tread the verge of Jordan,
Bid my anxious fears subside;
Death of death and hell's destruction,
Land me safe on Canaan's side.
Songs of praises, songs of praises
I will ever give to Thee;
I will ever give to Thee.

(*LSB* 918)

Prayer

O Lord, who has called us out of darkness into Your marvelous light, we pray for the light of truth that only You can reveal to us. Open Your Holy Word to us and grant us the insight of the Holy Spirit so that we may use that Word to grow in faith toward You and love toward our neighbor. As we follow Your ancient people Israel into the wilderness during their forty years of wandering, guide us also with Your powerful hand, dealing with us not after our sins but according to Your mercy in Christ. Amen.

Digging Deep
My Personal Study for Week 1

Day 1 • Skim Exodus 12; read Numbers 9:1–14

1. What actions were the signs of faith that God gave to the Israelites to do at the first Passover (Exodus 12)?

2. Recall the recurrence of "evening and . . . morning" in Genesis 1. Why is it significant that the Passover meal ritual is begun "at twilight" (Exodus 12:6; Numbers 9:3, 5; 1 Corinthians 11:23–24)?

3. What was the practical (Exodus 12:39) and theological (Exodus 12:19–20; 1 Corinthians 5:6–8) significance of unleavened bread?

4. What do you think would have been the most vivid memories for the Israelites to recall upon celebrating the first few Passover festivals (see Exodus 12:14)?

5. What sort of judgments would the Lord pass on the gods of Egypt (Exodus 12:12)? Consult also Deuteronomy 32:16–18 and 1 Corinthians 10:18–22; how would this judgment apply to us Christians?

Day 2 • Read Exodus 23:20–33; Numbers 13–14

6. Read Genesis 15. What were the two key features of God's promised inheritance to Abraham?

7. What commandment is emphasized in Exodus 23:20–33? How are the Israelites to demonstrate their faith in the Lord?

8. What is the wisdom of driving out the inhabitants of the Promised Land "little by little" (Exodus 23:29–30)?

9. Read Numbers 13. What is the root cause of the forty years of wandering in the wilderness? Who will endure this time of testing? Can you spot the irony?

10. Numbers 14:18 is repeated often in the Old Testament—it could be considered a type of miniature creed. What is its central truth? Formulate a sentence of your own that reflects your understanding of this same truth of Scripture.

Day 3 • Skim Exodus 16–17; read Numbers 11

11. What was the occasion that led to the Lord's giving manna to the people of Israel? What was the spiritual teaching that accompanied the gift of manna, according to Deuteronomy 8:3?

Making Offerings

Distribute before session 2 for use in session 2.
Use enrichment magazine pp. 8–10.

Leviticus 1–5; Numbers 28–29

Resources for Worship

Use these resources for your daily study at home and at the week's assembly.

Hymn

We give Thee but Thine own,
Whate'er the gift may be;
All that we have is Thine alone,
A trust, O Lord, from Thee.

May we Thy bounties thus
As stewards true receive
And gladly, as Thou blessest us,
To Thee our firstfruits give!

Oh, hearts are bruised and dead,
And homes are bare and cold,
And lambs for whom the Shepherd bled
Are straying from the fold.

To comfort and to bless,
To find a balm for woe,
To tend the lone and fatherless
Is angels' work below.

The captive to release,
To God the lost to bring,
To teach the way of life and peace,
It is a Christ-like thing.

And we believe Thy Word,
Though dim our faith may be:
Whate'er for Thine we do, O Lord,
We do it unto Thee.

(*LSB* 781)

Prayer

Almighty God, You are pleased with the offerings and worship of lowly men because of the perfect sacrifice of Christ. Grant us humble faith to offer before You our sincerest thanks and praise so that we may not fall to the temptation to take Your love for granted. As we see the various offerings presented to You by the children of Israel, make our lives as a pleasing aroma before Your presence and a worthy confession of what our Lord has done for us. In His name we pray. Amen.

Digging Deep
My Personal Study for Week 2

Day 1 • Read Leviticus 1; Numbers 28:1–10

1. What animals are the options for the burnt offering? In what order do you suppose they are given in Leviticus 1?

2. What extra ceremony is explicitly noted along with offering a bull for a burnt offering?

3. Describe the role of the priest and the role of the man offering the burnt offering. What changes are made in these roles depending on the animal used?

4. In Leviticus, God is now speaking to Moses, not on top of a mountain, but at the tent as His dwelling. Read John 1:11–14. What has replaced the tent as the Lord's speaking and dwelling place?

5. Read Numbers 28:1–10. Why would the Lord consider a burnt offering as a "pleasing aroma" or as a "food offering"? Compare with John 1:29. With what sacrifice is God pleased?

Day 2 • Read Leviticus 2; Numbers 28:11–15

6. What makes the offerings in Leviticus 2 different from those described in chapter 1? Can you pick out any similarities?

7. Who eats the grain offerings that are dedicated to the Lord? What other actions are done to indicate that these offerings are holy?

8. When was the offering of firstfruits commanded to be given? How is the firstfruits idea applied to our situation today as Christians?

9. Didn't Cain make an offering of grain or another kind of crop? See Genesis 4 and Hebrews 11:4. What is the deciding factor when the Lord regards someone's offering?

10. Read Psalm 50:7–23. What abuse of sacrifices is criticized in this passage? What is preferred above all sacrifices and ceremonies? What is the danger of feigning faith?

Day 3 • Read Leviticus 3

11. Point out similarities and differences between peace (or fellowship) offerings here in chapter 3 and the burnt offerings discussed in chapter 1.

Priestly Ministry

Distribute before session 3 for use in session 3.
Use enrichment magazine pp. 11–13.

Leviticus 6–10; Numbers 3–4; 12; 15; 18–19; Deuteronomy 12–13

Resources for Worship

Use these resources for your daily study at home and at the week's assembly.

Hymn

See, the Lord ascends in triumph;
Conqu'ring King in royal state,
Riding on the clouds, His chariot,
To His heav'nly palace gate.
Hark! The choirs of angel voices
Joyful alleluias sing,
And the portals high are lifted
To receive their heav'nly King.

Who is this that comes in glory
With the trump of jubilee?
Lord of battles, God of armies,
He has gained the victory.
He who on the cross did suffer,
He who from the grave arose,
He has vanquished sin and Satan;
He by death has crushed His foes.

While He lifts His hands in blessing,
He is parted from His friends;
While their eager eyes behold Him,
He upon the clouds ascends.
He who walked with God and pleased Him,
Preaching truth and doom to come,
He, our Enoch, is translated
To His everlasting home.

Now our heav'nly Aaron enters
With His blood within the veil;
Joshua now is come to Canaan,
And the kings before Him quail.
Now He plants the tribes of Israel
In their promised resting place;
Now our great Elijah offers
Double portion of His grace.

He has raised our human nature
On the clouds to God's right hand;
There we sit in heav'nly places,
There with Him in glory stand.
Jesus reigns, adored by angels;
Man with God is on the throne.
By our mighty Lord's ascension
We by faith behold our own.

(*LSB* 494)

Prayer

Eternal God, You granted Aaron and his priestly sons access to Your earthly throne of grace in order to offer the sacrifice for the sins of the people. Now that You have made all Christians to be Your royal priests, welcome us into Your kingdom and teach us to pray with boldness and confidence, that no adversity in this life may rob us of the promised inheritance that is already ours in the life to come; through Jesus Christ our Lord. Amen.

Digging Deep
My Personal Study for Week 3

Day 1 • Read Leviticus 7; Numbers 3–4

1. What portions of the sacrifices are the priests allowed to eat? Which portions are forbidden? What is done with those instead?

2. Take note of the numbering of days in Leviticus 7:16–18 concerning the freewill offering. What parallel could be drawn from this to Good Friday and Easter?

3. What was Aaron's role with Moses while the Israelites were still in Egypt (Exodus 7)? What changes would be made once the people entered the wilderness?

4. What distinctions are drawn between Aaron's sons, the rest of the tribe of Levi, and all of the people belonging to the other tribes? What are their privileges and worship roles?

5. How do the holy things (altar, ark of the covenant, sacred vessels) get transported if they cannot be seen or touched? Who is placed in charge of them specifically at this time?

Day 2 • Read Leviticus 6; 9; Numbers 18–19

6. Leviticus 6:8–7:18 seems like it is a repetition of everything from chapters 1–5. Is this just a summary? If not, what else is added in these directions that wasn't included earlier?

7. Name one reason why the fire was kept going on the altar of burnt offering. Can you think of a practical reason as well as a theological reason?

8. Why do the priests and Levites get to eat so much food, including meat?

9. The Levites are set aside to serve the priests, who are the ones put in charge of the Old Testament worship. What personality types do you think would be compatible with this job description? Which ones would be less compatible?

10. Read 1 Peter 2:9–12 and 1 Timothy 2:1–6. How is the Christian's role as a royal priest similar and different as compared with the duties of the Old Testament priests and Levites?

Clean and Unclean

Distribute before session 4 for use in session 4.
Use enrichment magazine pp. 14–16.

Leviticus 11–15; Numbers 5; 19; Deuteronomy 14; Luke 2

Resources for Worship

Use these resources for your daily study at home and at the week's assembly.

Hymn

If Your belovèd Son, O God,
Had not to earth descended
And in our mortal flesh and blood
Had not sin's power ended,
Then this poor, wretched soul of mine
In hell eternally would pine
Because of my transgression.

All righteousness by works is vain;
The Law brings condemnation.
True righteousness by faith I gain;
Christ's work is my salvation.
His death, that perfect sacrifice,
Has paid the all-sufficient price;
In Him my hope is anchored.

My guilt, O Father, You have laid
On Christ, Your Son, my Savior.
Lord Jesus, You my debt have paid
And gained for me God's favor.
O Holy Spirit, Fount of grace,
The good in me to You I trace;
In faith and hope preserve me.

(*LSB* 568:1, 4, 5)

Prayer

Heavenly Father, we are unclean due to our debilitating and disfiguring sin. As You provided for healing and cleansing for those who in ancient Israel were ceremonially unclean, so too in our day, cleanse and purify our hearts with Your Holy Gospel to the end so that we may with true and lasting faith enter Your kingdom and stand on Your holy ground. In the name of Jesus we pray. Amen.

Digging Deep
My Personal Study for Week 4

Day 1 • Read Leviticus 11; Deuteronomy 14

1. What are the differentiating features that clarify which animals are clean and which are unclean? Were hares and rock badgers considered clean or unclean? Why?

2. Why does the Lord speak now to both Moses and Aaron (Leviticus 11:1)? Skim the rest of the book to note how often the chapter and section headings include both names.

3. In Leviticus 11:32–38, where would the people encounter the unclean animals and undergo purification rituals if not in the courtyard of the tabernacle?

4. In what ways does our worship of the Lord today extend beyond the walls of our church?

5. How would staying away from unclean things be a demonstration of an Israelite's faith? What sort of things could be considered "unclean" for us today—in the sense that they get in the way of our access to God's gracious presence?

Day 2 • Read Leviticus 12; Luke 2:22–39

6. What are the requirements for purification after childbirth? What distinctions are made?

7. The two offerings that are required to be presented before the tent of meeting are a burnt offering and a sin offering. Which would you expect to be given to the Lord on the occasion of a birth?

8. In the account of the presentation of Jesus in the temple in Luke 2:22–24, how old was Jesus at this time, and what is the significance of the offering that Mary and Joseph gave in fulfillment of this ritual?

9. Review the portion of this study that addressed the topic of blood. How is it mentioned in the purification following childbirth?

10. Describe the process in Leviticus 12 of the three stages of this rite of passage: separation from the community, transition period for the mother, rite of reincorporation into the community. How would this process underline for a woman the importance of her role as bearer of children?

Atonement

Distribute before session 5 for use in session 5.
Use enrichment magazine pp. 17–19.

Leviticus 16–17; 21; 23; Numbers 29; Matthew 6; Hebrews; 1 John 2

Resources for Worship

Use these resources for your daily study at home and at the week's assembly.

Hymn

Salvation unto us has come
  By God's free grace and favor;
Good works cannot avert our doom,
  They help and save us never.
Faith looks to Jesus Christ alone,
Who did for all the world atone;
  He is our one Redeemer.

What God did in His Law demand
  And none to Him could render
Caused wrath and woe on ev'ry hand
  For man, the vile offender.
Our flesh has not those pure desires
The spirit of the Law requires,
  And lost is our condition.

It was a false, misleading dream
  That God His Law had given
That sinners could themselves redeem
  And by their works gain heaven.
The Law is but a mirror bright
To bring the inbred sin to light
  That lurks within our nature.

From sin our flesh could not abstain,
  Sin held its sway unceasing;
The task was useless and in vain,
  Our guilt was e'er increasing.
None can remove sin's poisoned dart
Or purify our guileful heart—
  So deep is our corruption.

Yet as the Law must be fulfilled
  Or we must die despairing,
Christ came and has God's anger stilled,
  Our human nature sharing.
He has for us the Law obeyed
And thus the Father's vengeance stayed
  Which over us impended.

Since Christ has full atonement made
  And brought to us salvation,
Each Christian therefore may be glad
  And build on this foundation.
Your grace alone, dear Lord, I plead,
Your death is now my life indeed,
  For You have paid my ransom.
(*LSB* 555:1–6)

Prayer

Lord Jesus Christ, our atonement sacrifice and advocate before the Father, we thank You for Your selfless self-offering for our sakes, and we praise You for Your full completion of the salvation task. Assure us of Your presence with us to the very end of the age, and fix our eyes both on Your cross, where our atonement was achieved, and on Your Holy Supper, where we find our atonement handed out for our benefit. Amen.

Digging Deep
My Personal Study for Week 5

Day 1 • Read Leviticus 16; 23:23–32; Numbers 29:7–11

1. What animals are sacrificed on the Day of Atonement? Why is one goat allowed to live?

2. What is the intended outcome for the Day of Atonement ceremonies? How is this different from the sin offerings that are presented every other day?

3. Use a concordance or Bible dictionary to look up the words *atone, atonement,* and *propitiation*; read some of the Scriptures that have these words. What other synonyms can you find? What is taking place in the majority of these Bible passages?

4. If sins are forgiven in the atonement sacrifice, why does the scapegoat (or "Azazel") also take away the peoples' sins when it is released into the wilderness?

5. How can you use the Day of Atonement ritual to explain to someone why there were so many different sacrifices and liturgical rules in ancient Israel?

Day 2 • Read Leviticus 17:1–9

6. Why is the tabernacle or tent of meeting the only appropriate place to sacrifice an animal as an offering to the Lord?

7. Read 1 Chronicles 13:8–13. For what reason was the man named Uzzah killed? What did King David do in response?

8. Where are the tabernacle and its courtyard located in relation to the Israelite camp? How will this arrangement change once they arrive in the Promised Land? See Exodus 33:7–11; Numbers 2; Deuteronomy 12:5–7; and Joshua 18:1.

9. In Leviticus 17:7, God specifically denounces offering sacrifices to goat demons. From what danger is He preserving His people? Refer also to Deuteronomy 32:17; 2 Chronicles 11:15; Isaiah 13:21; and 1 Corinthians 10:20–21.

Holiness

Distribute before session 6 for use in session 6.
Use enrichment magazine pp. 21–22.

Leviticus 17–22; Numbers 6; Deuteronomy 7; 9; 17–18; 21; 24–25

Resources for Worship

Use these resources for your daily study at home and at the week's assembly.

Hymn

Immortal, invisible,
God only wise,
In light inaccessible
hid from our eyes,
Most blessèd, most glorious,
the Ancient of Days,
Almighty, victorious,
Thy great name we praise.

Unresting, unhasting,
and silent as light,
Nor wanting, nor wasting,
Thou rulest in might;
Thy justice like mountains
high soaring above
Thy clouds which are fountains
of goodness and love.

To all life Thou givest—
to both great and small—
In all life Thou livest,
the true Life of all;
We blossom and flourish
as leaves on the tree
And wither and perish—
but naught changes Thee.

Great Father of glory,
pure Father of light,
Thine angels adore Thee,
all veiling their sight;
All laud we would render:
O help us to see
'Tis only the splendor
of light that hides Thee.

(*LSB* 802)

Prayer

O righteous God, without whom nothing is holy, deal with us not as our sins deserve but according to Your never-ending mercy. May Your holiness not only convict us of our trespasses but also enrich us with pardon and peace. Grant us Your Holy Spirit, that our bodies may be sanctified to be Your temple and Your holy love fill us with service toward our neighbor, not as though we were mere people-pleasers but as we do good works that are acceptable in Your sight; through Jesus Christ, our Lord, we pray. Amen.

Digging Deep
My Personal Study for Week 6

Day 1 • Read Leviticus 17:10–16; Deuteronomy 7:1–16; 21:1–9

1. What are the consequences for the person who disobeys the prohibition against eating blood?

2. How does this punishment compare with the blessing given in Numbers 6:22–27?

3. Why would the Lord give the command to destroy the nations of the Promised Land completely? In what way do these nations belong to God in His wrath?

4. How would you respond to the atonement process given in Deuteronomy 21:1–9 if it was your family member who was murdered by an unknown assailant? In what promises would your comfort lie?

5. Read Acts 15:4–21. Why would eating blood still be prohibited among Christians of the New Testament? Would this continue indefinitely?

Day 2 • Read Leviticus 18; Deuteronomy 24–25

6. Based on the introduction to Leviticus 18 (vv. 1–5), why does the Lord spell out specific sexual practices that the Israelites must avoid?

7. What does it mean for the land to "vomit you out" (Leviticus 18:28), and what connection do these consequences have with God's gift of land for His people?

8. Survey the biblical examples of rival wives in Genesis 16; 21:8–13; 29:9–30:24; 1 Samuel 1:1–20. What were the negative consequences of these arrangements that departed from God's pattern for marriage?

9. What are the conditions in which a divorce is permitted under Old Testament civil law in Deuteronomy 24:1–4?

10. Compare the levirate marriage requirements in Deuteronomy 25:5–10 with the procedure described in Ruth 4:1–12. What had changed in a century or two, and what remained similar?

Festivals

Distribute before session 7 for use in session 7.
Use enrichment magazine pp. 23–25.

Leviticus 23–25; Deuteronomy 15–16

Resources for Worship

Use these resources for your daily study at home and at the week's assembly.

Hymn

The God of Abr'ham praise,
  Who reigns enthroned above;
Ancient of everlasting days
  And God of love.
Jehovah, great I AM!
  By earth and heav'n confessed;
I bow and bless the sacred name
  Forever blest.

The God of Abr'ham praise,
  At whose supreme command
From earth I rise and seek the joys
  At His right hand.
I all on earth forsake,
  Its wisdom, fame, and pow'r,
And Him my only portion make,
  My shield and tow'r.

The God of Abr'ham praise,
  Whose all-sufficient grace
Shall guide me all my pilgrim days
  In all my ways.
He deigns to call me friend;
  He calls Himself my God.
And He shall save me to the end
  Through Jesus' blood.

He by Himself has sworn;
  I on His oath depend.
I shall, on eagle wings upborne,
  To heav'n ascend.
I shall behold His face;
  I shall His pow'r adore
And sing the wonders of His grace
  Forevermore.

Though nature's strength decay,
  And earth and hell withstand,
To Canaan's bounds I urge my way
  At His command.
The wat'ry deep I pass,
  With Jesus in my view,
And through the howling wilderness
  My way pursue.

The goodly land I see,
  With peace and plenty blest:
A land of sacred liberty
  And endless rest.
There milk and honey flow,
  And oil and wine abound,
And trees of life forever grow
  With mercy crowned.

(*LSB* 798:1–6)

Prayer

O Blessed, Holy Trinity, Your Church celebrates Your mighty acts of salvation throughout the year. Although our seasons and celebrations have changed over time, continue to kindle in us a strong faith that is not titillated by quickly passing fashion but longs to be fed with the sincere milk of the Word. Lead us to see Christ in every festival of Israel and now as our teacher, host, and food in the Divine Services of which we are privileged to partake in our time. In Jesus' name we pray. Amen.

Digging Deep
My Personal Study for Week 7

Day 1 • Read Leviticus 23:1–3; 25:1–7; Deuteronomy 15

1. What features does the Sabbath hold in common with the yearly festivals that are described in Leviticus 23?

2. To what greater rest does the ritual of the Sabbath point, according to Hebrews 4:1–12?

3. If a Bible interpreter who wanted to accommodate evolutionary theory insisted that the six "days" of creation in Genesis 1 were really six "eras" of millions of years, how would that twisting of Scripture affect passages like Leviticus 23:3?

4. What point was Jesus proving by healing people on the Sabbath Day, even though He knew the Jewish authorities would use it against Him? For one of several examples, check Mark 2:23–28.

5. Why was the day of rest and worship moved from the Sabbath (Saturday) to Sunday? Refer to Luke 24:1; John 20:1, 19; Acts 20:7; and Revelation 1:10.

Day 2 • Read Leviticus 23:4–8; Deuteronomy 16:1–8

6. According to Leviticus 23:8, what has been added to the seven-day Feast of Unleavened Bread (Passover)?

7. What makes the Passover meal a remembrance of a past event and, at the same time, a participation in it?

8. Review the following mentions of Passover in the Gospels: Luke 2:41; John 2:13; 6:4; 12:1; Matthew 26:17. Why is the festival important to the written account of Jesus' ministry and teaching?

9. Compare the Lord's Supper to the Passover meal. What is different? the same? Why is it offered more frequently than once a year?

By the "Numbers"

Distribute before session 8 for use in session 8.
Use enrichment magazine pp. 27–29.

Numbers 1–2; 16–17; 20–26; 31; Deuteronomy 31; 34; 2 Kings 18

Resources for Worship

Use these resources for your daily study at home and at the week's assembly.

Hymn

Come, you faithful, raise the strain
Of triumphant gladness!
God has brought His Israel
Into joy from sadness,
Loosed from Pharaoh's bitter yoke
Jacob's sons and daughters,
Led them with unmoistened foot
Through the Red Sea waters.

'Tis the spring of souls today:
Christ has burst His prison
And from three days' sleep in death
As a sun has risen;
All the winter of our sins,
Long and dark, is flying
From His light, to whom is giv'n
Laud and praise undying.

Now the queen of seasons, bright
With the day of splendor,
With the royal feast of feasts
Comes its joy to render;
Comes to gladden faithful hearts
Which with true affection
Welcome in unwearied strain
Jesus' resurrection!

For today among His own
Christ appeared, bestowing
His deep peace, which evermore
Passes human knowing.
Neither could the gates of death
Nor the tomb's dark portal
Nor the watchers nor the seal
Hold Him as a mortal.

Alleluia! Now we cry
To our King immortal,
Who, triumphant, burst the bars
Of the tomb's dark portal.
Come, you faithful, raise the strain
Of triumphant gladness!
God has brought His Israel
Into joy from sadness!

(*LSB* 487)

Prayer

Blessed Lord, You brought Your people Israel up to the very last years of their wilderness wandering by a mighty and outstretched arm. Break and hinder, we pray, every evil counsel and will of the devil, the world, and our sinful nature, those enemies who oppose us in our spiritual walk under the shelter of Your salvation. Grant us Your steadfast protection, that we may ever give thanks to You, for Your love and mercy truly endure forever. Amen.

Digging Deep
My Personal Study for Week 8

Day 1 • Read Numbers 1–2; 26

1. Compare the three censuses: Exodus 30:11–16; Numbers 1–2; Numbers 26. How did they change from one to the next? What was the express purpose of each?

2. Why were the Levites excluded from the census? Skim Numbers 3. How would their numbers be counted differently from the rest of the Israelites and for what purpose?

3. If the tribe of Levi was excluded, how did the tribes still end up numbering twelve? Why is this number significant in the Bible?

4. How are each tribe's camps arranged around the tent of meeting, and as they march? Compare this to Jacob's arrangement of his family caravan in Genesis 33:1–3.

5. How does Judah's role as lead tribe point forward to Christ? Consult other passages about this son of Jacob: Genesis 38; 43:3–9; 49:8–10.

Day 2 • Read Numbers 16–17

6. What was Korah's objection against Moses and Aaron? What did he desire for himself and the whole congregation of Israel?

7. How did Moses and Aaron respond to this challenge to their authority?

8. What is the significance of the budding staff of Aaron? Why will it be kept inside the ark of the covenant?

9. What are the responsibilities of a Christian congregation's laity? of their pastor?

10. If you were to experience a time of conflict between a congregation and pastor, how would you respond? To what Scripture passages or additional resources would you turn to for help?

Planning to Settle

Distribute before session 9 for use in session 9.
Use enrichment magazine pp. 30–32.

Leviticus 26–27; Numbers 13; 32–36; Deuteronomy 1–4; 9–11; 19–34

Resources for Worship

Use these resources for your daily study at home and at the week's assembly.

Hymn

O day of rest and gladness,
  O day of joy and light,
O balm of care and sadness,
  Most beautiful, most bright;
This day the high and lowly,
  Through ages joined to bless,
Sing, "Holy, holy, holy,"
  The triune God confess.

This day at earth's creation
  The light first had its birth;
This day for our salvation
  Christ rose from depths of earth;
This day our Lord victorious
  The Spirit sent from heav'n,
And thus this day most glorious
  A threefold light was giv'n.
(*LSB* 906:1–2)

Prayer

O God and Father of our Lord Jesus Christ, in Your love and mercy, You delivered Your people from forty years in the desert and finally brought them under Your servant Joshua to the land of their promised inheritance. Help and guide us constantly in our spiritual journey, for we know not where we go; however, by grace, we are confident that You are there with us, with Your everlasting arms underneath us. Lead us from our sin to the cross; to the empty tomb; to the pulpit, font, and altar; and finally, to our grave. At every turn, help us witness to Your love and instruction, as well as testify to Your forgiveness and everlasting peace; through the same Jesus Christ, Your Son, our Lord. Amen.

Digging Deep
My Personal Study for Week 9

Day 1 • Read Numbers 13; 32; Deuteronomy 3

1. What request did the people from the tribes of Reuben and Gad bring to Moses? Why did they ask this?

2. What was Moses' reaction to this request? What was the previous incident like this that had prevented Israel from entering Canaan?

3. What was the agreement reached in Numbers 32? Why was only half of the tribe of Manasseh included with Reuben and Gad?

4. Read Joshua 22. Was the agreement kept? What was the purpose for the altar that they called Witness?

5. Why do you think it is important to keep vows made to God and fellow people, even though we are not required to make them at all? What bad effects can there be if a freely made promise is subsequently broken? Can you come up with any contemporary examples?

Day 2 • Read Numbers 33; skim Deuteronomy 1–4; 9–11

6. What is listed in Numbers 33? Why would Moses include this at a point just before Israel entered into the Promised Land?

7. Reread Deuteronomy 6. How does Israel's history relate to the commandments that are to be passed on to future generations? What will that history contribute to their confession of faith?

8. Almost the entire Book of Deuteronomy is an extended quote. Who is speaking? Why is most of the material repeated from earlier books of the Pentateuch?

9. In a similar way as Deuteronomy, Chronicles repeats Israel's history and uses it as an instruction for future generations. Compare 2 Kings 21 with 2 Chronicles 33. Now see the differences between Exodus 20 and Deuteronomy 5. What is being emphasized in each later version?

10. Review Psalm 136 and the history that it retells in its liturgical form. Find another psalm that similarly recounts events from the exodus and wanderings in the wilderness. What teaching does the psalm use from that event as a basis for praise and prayer?

Day 3 • Read Numbers 34–36; Deuteronomy 19–20; 26

11. According to Numbers 33:50–56, how will the land be divided among the tribes? How is the census in chapter 26 going to figure in?

12. Read Deuteronomy 19:14 and 27:17. What is sinful about moving a property landmark? What would be a comparable offense in modern times?

13. Where will the Levites live in relation to other Israelite tribes, if they do not have their own section of land?

14. What is the function of a city of refuge? What are the limitations placed on exacting vengeance for the shedding of blood?

15. Which is better: a required tithe or a freewill offering? Which will more likely yield more giving? Can the concept of a tithe be incorporated into a Christian's giving, but without making it into a law-oriented obligation? If so, how?

Day 4 • Read Leviticus 26–27; Deuteronomy 21; 27–29

16. What are the two key sections of Leviticus 26 and Deuteronomy 28? How do these chapters relate to the rest of God's covenant with Israel?

17. Describe the progression of the stages by which Israel will receive consequences for their disobedience in Leviticus 26:14–33.

18. How does the curse in Deuteronomy 21:22–23 relate to Christ? What happens to the curse of our sin when we believe in Him?

19. What does the repeated response "Amen" mean in Deuteronomy 27:15–26?

20. Refer to Deuteronomy 29:18–21 and Hebrews 12:15. What sort of sin characterizes a person as a "root bearing poisonous or bitter fruit" among believers? Why cannot psychology alone explain the actions of such an antagonist?

Day 5 • Read Deuteronomy 30–34

21. Compare Deuteronomy 30:11–14 with Romans 10:5–13. If it is true that the Law condemns us, and that it is impossible to fulfill God's commandments perfectly, then in what way is it "not too hard"?

22. What is the purpose of the song in Deuteronomy 32 that the Lord commanded Moses to teach to the Israelites?

23. Choose one of the twelve tribes and compare and contrast its blessing from Moses in Deuteronomy 33 with its blessing from Jacob in Genesis 49.

24. Read Luke 9:28–36. When was Moses finally allowed to be in the Promised Land? What is the irony of this opportunity that was given to him?

25. The three biblical books we have studied in this course are typically regarded as very confusing and full of meaningless repetitive lists. In the last few weeks, how has your understanding and appreciation for this section of Scripture changed? Of the material we covered, what would you be able to explain better to others?

Day 3 • Read Numbers 20; Deuteronomy 31; 34

11. What were the circumstances of Moses' act of disobedience that kept him from leading the Israelites into the Promised Land?

12. What were the differences between this incident and the one recorded in Exodus 17:1–7?

13. How is Joshua going to receive God's Word and will as Israel's leader? What makes this procedure different from how Moses communicated with the Lord? (see Numbers 27:18–23).

14. What is communicated in the ceremony of the laying on of hands? How is it used today among Christians?

15. Read John 1:17 and Romans 8:1–3. Scripture associates the Law with Moses, since he wrote down God's Law and the Ten Commandments. How does the story of Moses' disobedience teach us that the Law cannot save us?

Day 4 • Read Numbers 21; 2 Kings 18:1–8

16. Why did the Lord send the plague of "fiery" serpents against the people of Israel?

17. What did the Lord have Moses do to save the people who were bitten by the serpents?

18. Read John 3:14–16. What similarity is there between the bronze serpent and Jesus? Why do you suppose Jesus uses this analogy in explaining saving faith to Nicodemus?

19. Why did King Hezekiah destroy the bronze serpent? About how many years had passed since the time of Moses?

20. What does it mean to look up to Christ in faith? Why is it insufficient for a Christian only to follow Jesus' example of virtuous living?

Day 5 • Read Numbers 21–25; 31

21. Where are the kingdoms of the Amorite rulers Sihon and Og located?

22. How do these military victories fulfill the prophecy of Genesis 15:16?

23. What was Balak's reason for hiring the services of the prophet Balaam?

24. What were the limitations that God placed on Balaam's task? How was his donkey involved?

25. Why was the angel of the Lord addressed in the same way as God? How does this compare with other biblical encounters with this angel? See Genesis 22:15–18; Exodus 3:2–6; Judges 13:8–22.

10. How does a background knowledge of the Passover and other Israelite festivals help you understand Christian observances like Good Friday and Easter? See 1 Corinthians 5:6–8; Colossians 2:8–17; Hebrews 10:20; 13:10–16.

Day 3 • Read Leviticus 23:9–22; Deuteronomy 16:9–12

11. What does *firstfruits* mean? What significance does it have for the Israelites to refrain from eating food from their harvest until their firstfruits offering has been presented?

12. What is a proper Christian attitude of stewardship toward the things that God has given to us? How does the firstfruits ceremony teach us this truth today? (See Psalm 116:12–14.)

13. The Feast of Weeks is known as Pentecost, from the Greek for "fifty." What are the differences in the offerings made before and after the seven-week interval?

14. The firstfruits were offered on the day after the Passover Sabbath (Leviticus 23:11). This would have been the same day that Jesus rose from the dead. How does Paul relate Christ's resurrection to the firstfruits festival in 1 Corinthians 15:16–23?

15. How was the Pentecost festival related to harvest time in the Old Testament? What sort of harvest was begun in the Christian Church on Pentecost (Acts 2)?

Day 4 • Read Leviticus 23:23–25, 33–44; Deuteronomy 16:13–17

16. What ceremony began the seventh month of the year? What made this month distinct from the others?

17. Two different kinds of trumpets are listed in Psalm 98:6 and 2 Chronicles 15:14. What function do both the rams' horns and silver bugles serve? See Exodus 19:16; Numbers 10:1–10; Joshua 6:1–16; 1 Kings 1:32–37; Ezekiel 33:1–9. Consult a few different translations to help you.

18. What is the purpose of lodging in booths for the seven days of the festival (Leviticus 23:33–43)? Of what would this remind us Christians today?

19. The Hebrew and Arabic words for "pilgrimage" are very similar. Compare and contrast the pilgrimage at the Israelite Festival of Booths with the Muslim pilgrimage to Mecca. What is done instead of the Day of Atonement in Islam?

20. Read John 1:14. How did the Son of God dwell ("tabernacle," as in a booth) among us on earth? What relationship would this have to the tearing of the temple curtain at Jesus' death?

Day 5 • Read Leviticus 25

21. How was the land dedicated to the Lord during the Sabbath year? How did the people eat during this time?

22. What are the additional observances when the jubilee year arrives?

23. Who really owns the land, if an Israelite buys property from a fellow Israelite and then must return it at the jubilee? Why is the relationship more like a rental agreement?

24. What are exceptions to the jubilee transfer of property? What difference does it make if a home is inside a walled city or belongs to a Levite?

25. What is the Christian jubilee? See John 8:31–36; Hebrews 2:14–18; Romans 7:14–8:4; Philemon 8–20; Galatians 5:1.

Day 3 • Read Leviticus 19; Numbers 6

11. What is the significance of the repeated phrase "I am the LORD" throughout Leviticus 19?

12. What obligations would an Israelite believer have toward his neighbor? How do these pronouncements compare to the Ten Commandments?

13. How are the prohibitions in Leviticus 19:19 related to one another? Who was allowed to wear fabric made of two different kinds of material (see Exodus 28:6, 15)?

14. What would be the benefit, temporal or spiritual, in taking the vow of a Nazirite (Numbers 6)? How would it teach the Israelites about Christ?

15. Recall the story of Samson and Delilah in Judges 16. Why did Samson's hair seem to be the source of his strength? What was the true source?

Day 4 • Read Leviticus 20; 22; Deuteronomy 9:1–12; 17:1–7

16. What damage would there be if Israel were to participate in the Canaanites' worship of the god Molech?

17. How is God's free and undeserved grace toward Israel described in Deuteronomy 9:1–12?

18. What is the reason that the Lord gives for the inheritance of land that He gives to the Israelites? What will happen if they break faith with the Lord themselves?

19. How do the statutes of Deuteronomy 17:1–7 preserve the holiness of God's people?

20. How does the Church of today guard and promote God's gift of holiness?

Day 5 • Read Deuteronomy 18:15–22

21. What similarities to Moses will be repeated in the Prophet who is to come?

22. What is the test to show whether a prophet's words are the Word of the Lord or not?

23. See Acts 5:27–40. How did Gamaliel apply Moses' test convincingly for the Jewish Council at Paul's trial?

24. See Acts 17:10–12. What was the Bereans' practice when they heard the Gospel? If they had studied the books from the wilderness wanderings, what corroboration of Paul's message do you think they would have found there?

25. What does Paul require the Galatian (1:6–10) Christians to do concerning the different doctrines that were being taught them? Why were they prone to believe these other teachers?

10. Read 1 Samuel 4–5. What power accompanied the ark of the covenant? Why could the Philistines take it away when no one but the priests could even touch it?

Day 3 • Read Leviticus 21

11. What extra ceremonial duties does the high priest have on the Day of Atonement? What is allowed for him to do, and what is still forbidden?

12. The priest may participate in funeral rites only for his closest blood relatives (Leviticus 21:1–4). Why would he not even be eligible for the cleansing ritual? If he cannot bury his own wife, who would do it for him?

13. What is denied to those among Aaron's descendants who have blemishes or deformities? What are they allowed to do?

14. How does the physical condition of the high priest relate to the atonement duties that he performs? How does his condition relate to the ritual's fulfillment in Christ?

15. Read Matthew 10:37; 19:6–12; Luke 9:60; John 6:33; 1 Thessalonians 4:3; Hebrews 2:11; and Revelation 5:8. How do the activities, privileges, and demands on Old Testament priests compare to those of all Christians in the New Testament?

Day 4 • Read Hebrews 2; 5; 7–10; 1 John 2

16. Why was it important for Jesus to come to live, die, and rise again in our human flesh?

17. How does the priestly order of Melchizedek compare to the Levitical priesthood?

18. What distinction does the order of Melchizedek offer to the one sacrifice of Christ as opposed to the yearly sacrifices of the Old Testament high priest?

19. What priestly sacrifices do we now offer to the Lord, in Christ, for the sake of other people?

20. What would be the best response to someone who challenges that Jesus died for the sins of everyone in the world and asks, "If He did, then why won't everyone go to heaven?"

Day 5 • Read Leviticus 16:29–34; Matthew 6:16–18

21. How would fasting contribute to the Israelites' worship on the Day of Atonement?

22. Read Esther 4:1–3; Job 1:20–22; and Jonah 3:5–9. What other actions are done together with fasting? How do these instances of fasting differ with what was directed on the Day of Atonement?

23. Read Isaiah 58:1–10. What attitude toward fasting is being criticized? What is more preferable than making a show of fasting?

24. If the New Testament Church has no requirement for fasting, why does Jesus still encourage people to fast in secret?

25. Have you tried fasting before? What were considerations that you had to keep in mind? If, for any reason, you cannot abstain from food, what other voluntary forms of self-discipline would you try instead?

Day 3 • Read Leviticus 13; Numbers 5

11. How many different varieties of skin disease ("leprosy") are addressed in Leviticus 13? Where is the examination intended to take place? Why does the priest examine the disease?

12. What are the signs that the different diseases have in common? Are there any cases where the priest's pronouncement is surprising?

13. Read Luke 17:11–19. What would be a reason why Jesus would ask the lepers to show themselves to the priests? How would this demonstrate their faith?

14. Why would the Samaritan not have been admitted before the priest in the temple? What would be better than that privilege?

15. Leviticus 13:47–59 discusses the case of an unclean garment. How would the instructions here compare to clothing ourselves with Christ, as described in Galatians 3:27; Ephesians 4:22–24; and Colossians 3:9–14?

Day 4 • Read Leviticus 14

16. What are the two sets of sacrifices necessary for cleansing someone from a leprous disease?

17. What would be the significance of staining one bird with the blood of the other bird and then letting it go free? What are the two cleansing rituals that require this procedure?

18. Compare the application of blood and oil for cleansing with the ordination ritual that is described in Leviticus 8:22–29. What are some similarities and differences between the two rites?

19. Imagine that your house was declared unclean due to the presence of a disease or infection. What are the first three things that you would remove from it before the priest came over to examine it?

20. Read Matthew 2:11; 9:10–13; and Luke 19:5–10. How does Jesus cleanse an unclean house and the people inside it? What is the value of Christian house blessings?

Day 5 • Read Leviticus 15; Numbers 19

21. What are the ways in which a bodily discharge could transfer uncleanness?

22. What are the other occasions when the sacrifices used for impurity from bodily discharges would be offered (Leviticus 15:14, 29)?

23. Why is unclean status often removed in the evening?

24. Why would sexual sins or abuse leave a victim with the feeling of being unclean? How can the person feel purified and made whole again?

25. Survey Mark 5:25–34; Luke 7:37–50; and Luke 10:30–34. What happens when Jesus comes in contact with an unclean person?

Day 3 • Read Leviticus 8:14–30; Deuteronomy 12–13

11. Trace what blood signifies in the following verses: Genesis 4:10–11; 9:4–6; Exodus 7:17–19; 12:22–23; Ezekiel 33:6. What does it mean in each context?

12. Why would blood be considered important in the rites and ceremonies that are commanded in Leviticus?

13. Summarize the role of blood in the ordination of the priests. Where is blood applied in this rite? What would this say both to the priest and to the people watching?

14. Shedding the blood of animals is violent, yet it is also a part of everyday life, both now and 3,500 years ago. How do you make sense of this distinction, in light of our readings from both the Old and New Testaments?

15. What would your reaction be if you were to witness blood being used in this manner? If someone were to tell you that Christianity is only about happy thoughts or superstitions, what would you say in response?

Day 4 • Read Leviticus 8:1–13; Numbers 15:37–41; skim Exodus 28; 39

16. What is the item of priestly clothing that is most striking to you, and why? What would this signify both to the wearer and to the layman approaching the tabernacle?

17. What are the advantages to the use of vestments that testify to a particular holy calling or vocation? What would be the best way to address the risk of misappropriating them as a sign of power or control over others?

18. Read Revelation 7:9–17. What are the vestments depicted in this vision? Who wears them? What do they signify?

19. In Numbers 15:37–41, all the people have a symbolic item of clothing to wear. What does it stand for and how will it be used?

20. How do the priestly vestments of the Old Testament point the Christian to his or her status as a royal priest in the New Testament era? Who are the people we are to "remember" as we approach God on their behalf?

Day 5 • Read Leviticus 10; Numbers 12; 15

21. What led to the deaths of Aaron's sons Nadab and Abihu (Leviticus 10)?

22. Read about King Saul offering the sacrifice in 1 Samuel 13:5–14. Why did Samuel not accept Saul's reason for the exception? How does this compare to the consequences detailed in Leviticus and Numbers?

23. Read Acts 15:4–21. To what does Peter refer when he speaks about imposing a burden impossible to bear? How does this provide insight to liturgical ceremonies at the time of the beginning of the Christian Church?

24. Read the story of the Good Samaritan in Luke 10:25–37. What was the role of the priest and Levite in this narrative? What does this say, if anything, about serving the Lord in an Old Testament liturgical role?

25. What are the parallels between ritual desecration of holy items in worship in Leviticus 10 and 1 Corinthians 11:23–32? What is the reality behind the ceremony that remains in effect today?

12. What creates the "pleasing aroma" that arises before the Lord? See Genesis 8:20–22. What is it about the sacrifice that makes it pleasing to Him?

13. Read Ephesians 5:2; Hebrews 13:15–16; and Philippians 4:17–20. What is the "pleasing aroma" for our sacrifices to God in the New Testament Church?

14. See Genesis 9:3–7. Why are the Israelites prohibited from eating blood? What use is made of the fat that is found with the internal organs?

15. Even though sacrifices, ceremonial requirements, and prohibitions were fulfilled in Christ and were no longer binding on Christians in the New Testament, certain customs were kept for a while to minimize the giving of offense to weaker believers. See Acts 15:4–20. What are some issues of Christian freedom that you can think of that are appropriate to yield for the sake of the weak?

Day 4 • Read Leviticus 4; Numbers 29:31–34, 38

16. What needs to happen for the blood of the sin offering to be brought inside the tent of meeting to be sprinkled on the veil and the altar of incense? Why are the sins of the priest set apart from the sins of the rest of the people?

17. What is the function of the ash heap? Why is it located outside the Israelite camp?

18. How do the elders act on behalf of the whole people in the sin-offering ritual? What is done to assure forgiveness for the entire congregation?

19. In what way do the animals sacrificed correspond to the vocation of the one making the offering?

20. Note the reference to a sin offering in a portion of the Feast of Booths liturgy that appears in Numbers 29:31–34, 38. Why would this be done even if there is no particular unintentional sin that is confessed?

Day 5 • Read Leviticus 5

21. Why would refusing to speak in testimony be considered a ritual offense that would require a sin offering?

22. If flour is used as a substitute sin offering, why would oil and incense not be mixed in with it, as is the case with the grain offering of thanksgiving in Leviticus 2?

23. Making the guilt offering included providing "compensation" or a repayment of a debt. How does this proclaim Christ to the people, along with all the other sacrifices? Read Isaiah 53:10–11. How does Christ pay our debt?

24. Imagine you suddenly find yourself among the Israelites in the fifteenth century BC. Would you be comfortable participating in these sacrifices along with them? Why or why not?

25. What comes to your mind when you think of ritual? What is beneficial about it? What could be a drawback to having rituals?

12. Compare Exodus 16:35 with Joshua 5:10–12. When did the manna cease? How would its inherent lesson continue?

13. How did Moses get water to come from the rock the first time, in Exodus 17? How is faith involved in this episode? Refer to 1 Corinthians 10:1–13.

14. Read Numbers 11:10–15. How did the constant complaining of the Israelites affect Moses' interaction with the Lord?

15. Why can it be harmful to our faith to expect material blessings from God, when it is still true that all things come from His hand? Do we risk a punishment due to our lack of faith, as the Israelites suffered? Why or why not?

Day 4 • Skim Exodus 13; 26; 40; Numbers 7–9

16. Read Genesis 15:7–18; Exodus 14:19–20; 40:34–38; and Numbers 9:15–23. What does God use to signal His presence with His chosen people? What message does this appearance send to those who witness it?

17. Trace the "glory of the Lord" and the cloud in Exodus 33:17–23; 1 Kings 8:6–11; Isaiah 6:1–7; Ezekiel 1:4–28; Luke 9:34–36; and Acts 1:9–11. What would be fearful about this revelation of God?

18. Read Numbers 7:1–17. When the tabernacle is dedicated, the leaders of each tribe offer exactly the same gift, one each day. Note the tribe that begins this ceremony, and compare with Numbers 2:1–4 and Matthew 1:4. What is the significance of this priority?

19. According to Numbers 4:1–20, what is the special role of the Kohathite clan of the tribe of Levi? What are the limits of their service?

20. What would your reaction be if you were to witness a visible revealing of the glory of God? Are there advantages or disadvantages to our Lord being hidden in ordinary things for us in our day?

Day 5 • Read Exodus 20; Deuteronomy 5–8

21. Read Deuteronomy 5:1–21. Verse 6 (compare with Exodus 20:2) introduces the Ten Commandments. How would you describe the relationship between God and Israel that is set up by these words?

22. Read Deuteronomy 5:22–33. What was making the Israelites fearful of the Lord at this point, even though they were less so at other times (as implied by v. 29)?

23. According to Deuteronomy 6, what is the primary duty that Israelite parents are commanded to do for their children? What would be our equivalent duty today, and how would we perform it?

24. Read Deuteronomy 7. How would you describe the command to the Israelites that their enemies in the Promised Land be "devoted to destruction"? At what point did God put an end to this military policy?

25. Read Deuteronomy 8. How would these words of Moses help explain Jesus' statement, "How difficult it will be for those who have wealth to enter the kingdom of God!" (Mark 10:23)? What is the remedy provided to overcome this difficulty?

© Frank van den Bergh/iStockphoto.com

Our Safe Place

Safe places exist for a variety of people, including troubled youth, battered women, and homeless men. These places are found in fast-food restaurants, convenience stores, fire stations, libraries, and bus stations. Safe places connect needy people to immediate help and safety and often offer supportive services. Israelites had their own version of a safe place. They called them cities of refuge. These places were for "the manslayer who kills any person without intent" (Numbers 35:11). There were to be six safe havens, three "beyond the Jordan, and three cities in the land of Canaan" (Numbers 35:14). They are named in Joshua 20:7–8: Kedesh, Shechem, Hebron, Bezer, Ramoth, and Golan. This list of cities runs from north to south in Canaan and then south to north in the Transjordan. Spread out over the Promised Land, they were intended to be an ever-present help in trouble.

© Viadimir Piskunov/iStockphoto.com

© iStockphoto.com

An Ever-Present Help

The cities of refuge are not household names for us. For the uninitiated, they mean little or nothing, just a list. However, if you were on the run in ancient Israel, this list meant, well, it meant everything.

In Israelite culture, if someone in your family was killed, your relatives would call a meeting. Somebody would be appointed as a "avenger of blood" (see Numbers 35:19–27). This blood avenger was a representative from the family. He was to find the killer and release his neck from the burden of having to carry a head.

Admittedly, this was a bit crude, but it kept law and order. Of course, the major problem with such a system was an accidental death. Using Deuteronomy 19:5 as an example, a man goes into a forest with his neighbor to cut wood. As he swings his axe to chop down a tree, the axe's head flies off, hits his neighbor, and kills him. Now what happens? The dead man's family calls a meeting, and they appoint a blood avenger. And they don't choose rotund Uncle Earl. No, they pick fleet-footed cousin Nick. And Nick's orders are clear: "Chase the guy with the loose axe head and kill him!"

I bet you are saying, "That's not fair. He didn't *mean* to kill his neighbor!" You are right. But no one knew what else to do. No one, that is, except the Lord, the God of Israel. It is in His heart to provide cities of refuge all over the land to function as an ever-present help in trouble.

In the battle hymn of the Reformation, "A Mighty Fortress Is Our God" (*LSB* 656), Martin Luther describes the one chasing us with these phrases:

The old evil foe Now means deadly woe.

Though devils all the world should fill.

All eager to devour us.

This world's prince may still Scowl fierce as he will.

Deep guile and great might Are his dread arms in fight;

On earth is not his equal.

The avenger of blood comes to kill and steal and destroy. We see him in the rearview mirror. We feel his hot breath behind us. We know what it is like to run for our very lives!

As tempter, Satan chases after us, screaming, "Whatever it is you want to do, just do it. Are you angry? Act it out. Have some sexual fantasies? Go ahead, full throttle. Know some juicy gossip? Let it fly." As deceiver, he continues with these lies: "There are no limits, no consequences, and no responsibilities. Ready, set, go!"

When we give in to his temptations and deceptions, then, as accuser, he plants his foot on our necks and says, "Now that you said this, thought this, did this, drank this, smoked this, saw this, God is finished with you!" Satan, our adversary, prowls around like a roaring lion, looking to devour us.

© Jeff Chevrier/iStockphoto.com

Numbers 35 describes safe places for those who kill accidentally, unintentionally, and without premeditation. That leaves us out. Countless times we have sinned intentionally, with premeditation, and with malice aforethought. We are sitting ducks for the roaring lion! His strategy is clear: "I'll chase until I kill you!" And the corpses of beaten and battered Christians are all around to see. No one knows what to do, except the Lord, the God of Israel and the Father of our Lord Jesus Christ. It is in His heart to provide a refuge that is an ever-present help in times of trouble!

Old Testament cities of refuge are fulfilled in Him who is not only similar to but also greater than Joshua and Jonah, Melchizedek and Moses, the tabernacle and the temple. Israel's Scriptures testify to Him. Jesus Christ is God's final expression for a safe place, an asylum, a sanctuary, a haven, and a mighty fortress. "God is our refuge and strength, a very present help in trouble" (Psalm 46:1). So do not run aimlessly, hopelessly, or desperately. Run, rather, to the Refuge.

Help's Real Presence

Martin Luther was debating Christ's real presence in Holy Communion when he wrote these Latin words on a table: *Hoc est corpus meum* (Latin for "This is My body"). Jesus' true body and blood in the Eucharist is our ever-present help in trouble. By the power of God's Word, the forgiveness and mercy purchased for us on the cross is now present in, with, and under the bread and wine. Jesus gives us His real body and blood at the Table set before us in the presence of our enemy.

To the casual observer, this real present help in trouble must sound strange. We sing, "Holy, holy, holy Lord, Lord God of power and might," hear our pastor speak the Words of Institution, and approach the Table singing, "Lamb of God, You take away the sin of the world." It may look like a list of Israel's cities of refuge: Kedesh, Shechem, Hebron, Bezer, Ramoth, and Golan. But to the baptized, to the instructed, to those of us who know what it is like be tempted, deceived, accused, chased, and harassed, to those of us who know the run, this refuge, this gift, this liturgical list, means *everything*!

© Jan Will/iStockphoto.com

GOD LOVES A NOBODY

This is a warning. The article you are about to read is about nobody. It is not an article about everybody or anybody or even an article about somebody. Nope. This is an article about nobody.

The reason this article is about nobody is because of what Moses says about Israel, "You were the least of all the people" (Deuteronomy 7:7, author's translation). Israel was a lightweight and a loser. Israel was a nobody. The people had suffered as state slaves in Egypt for four hundred years. The Book of Numbers records their lackluster forty-year journey in the wilderness. Deuteronomy is Moses' farewell sermon. He reminds the Israelites that they have lived life unnoticed, in an average kind of hell. They were one huge, unnoticed nobody.

© Jan Will/iStockphoto.com

A Nobody for Nobodies

It takes one to know one. Moses had also washed out. He was a three-time loser. Strike 1: he takes matters into his own hands and murders an Egyptian. Strike 2: he tries to cover it up by hiding the dead man in the sand. Strike 3: hightailing it out of Egypt, Moses ends up in the Midian desert working for his father-in-law for forty years. Rather than being a hero, Moses ended up a being a big fat zero. Rather than looking forward, Moses looked back. And rather than dining with heads of state, Moses counted the heads of sheep. This is hardly what his friends wrote about him in his high school yearbook!

But then there was a voice and a burning bush and holy ground, and it all shocked the sandals right off his feet, literally. God chose, of all people, Moses! But if God chooses a nobody named Moses, why not choose the forty-year-old version instead of the eighty-year-old version? Moses at forty? Okay! Moses at eighty? No way! But benched at forty, Moses now at eighty is the Lord's first-round draft pick. His assignment? Get Israel out of Egypt.

As slaves in Egypt, Israel had no legal status, no worth, and no value. Their sons were murdered, tools of torture brought mayhem, and the daily quota of mud, bricks, and straw meant a life of monotony. But then there were frogs, flies, and fire. Then with a mighty hand and an outstretched arm, God chose, from all the nations, Israel!

It happened because Israel was the Lord's "treasured possession" (Deuteronomy 7:6). The Hebrew word is *segulah,* which denotes a one-of-a-kind treasure, someone's prized, priceless possession. A *segulah* is not loved because it is valuable. A *segulah* is valuable because it is loved.

Valuable because they are loved, Israel is called to treasure the Lord, the God of Abraham, Isaac, and Jacob. Rescued and redeemed, Israel is empowered to honor parents, protect life, cherish marriage, and place a high value on people's reputations and their property. Chosen as the Lord's *segulah,* Israel's mission to the world is to place an infinite value on the sorts of people society normally discards as nobodies: the orphan, the widow, and the alien at the gate.

Easier Said Than Done!

As Israel stands on the plains of Moab listening to the Book of Deuteronomy, they are about to enter the Promised Land. It is filled with enemies called Hittites, Amorites, Canaanites, Perizzites, Hivites, and Jebusites. These enemies tempted Israel into discounting everything. What God had called priceless—His Word, His covenants, His presence, and His steadfast love—was quickly discarded. Forgetting they were *segulah,* the nation was chewed up and spit out. Historians call it the destruction of Israel.

Jesus calls our enemy a liar and the father of lies. In the Book of Revelation, John calls him a destroyer and the ancient serpent who is the devil and Satan. Satan lives in our land, marking down God's treasures to cut-rate prices. This

happens all around us. Some men are in bondage to Internet pornography that horrifically cheapens God's gift of intimacy. Others discount their boss with burning bitterness. And still others build themselves up by putting other people down. There are women who sell their souls to the lord of the mall, the game of gossip, the jungle of judgment, and the silent stares. Others are striving for perfect bodies, so they find themselves fighting eating disorders, low self-esteem, and deep-running depression. Look at the carnage. Countless people are being chewed up and spit out. Historians call it the destruction of America.

Somebody Becomes Nobody

But Moses' burning bush and Israel's exodus were just the prelude, the first act, and the warm-up to another choosing, reclaiming, and redeeming. This plan of rescue also involved a Nobody who became "the least of all the people." Oh, don't get me wrong. At one point, He had been Somebody. Check that—He had been Mr. Somebody. John says, "All things were made through Him" (John 1:3). Paul proclaims, "He is the image of the invisible God" (Colossians 1:15). And the Hebrews writer says Jesus is "the radiance of the glory of God and the exact imprint of His nature" (Hebrews 1:3).

But Pharisees plot with Sadducees. Detractors say He is demon-possessed. The final assault begins with thirty pieces of silver, and He is sold away as a slave. Talk about getting trashed! In Gethsemane, Jesus loses all His friends. At Gabbatha, He loses the skin and muscle off His back. And at a hill called Golgotha, He loses the presence of His Father. Blood-soaked and spiked to wood, His lungs are screaming for air. Look again. Spit and sweat are caked to His cheeks. His lips are cracked and swollen. Stretched nerves threaten to snap as death twangs her morbid melody. Passersby mock Him: "This guy is one huge, unnoticed Nobody!"

Treasured Forever

It all ended: crucified, dead, and buried. Smell the odor of blood and the stench of death. Watch Joseph place Him in the tomb. See the confines, the darkness, the sealed stone.

And witness the charred marks of a divine explosion to life! There is nothing dead about our Jesus! Jesus blew the rock open from the inside and rolled away the stone. He surged out of the tomb and is still surging into the world to speak words straight from His heart to yours. Jesus says, "My dear *segulah*. No matter what, I will always love you!" This is no sentimental or syrupy love, but a fierce love for you—driven by nails, marked with scars, crowned with thorns, sealed in Holy Baptism, and delivered to you in the Holy Supper of His real body and blood. It all means you are not just anybody. You are more than just somebody. It means no one is an unnoticed nobody. That's not you. Not now, not ever. You are the Lord's *segulah*, His treasured possession, forever! "Thanks be to God for His inexpressible gift" (2 Corinthians 9:15).

Go to the *Land* I Will Show You

This is God's command to Abram. So the old man told his wife, Sarai, gathered his belongings, invited his nephew Lot, and then traveled to Canaan, the Promised Land. The world would never be the same! Israel's first moment of being settled in a land was when Jacob and his sons settled in Egypt under Joseph. They were given the best of the land and dwelled there in security and prosperity. Yet this was not *their* land. A pharaoh arose who forgot Joseph, and so he enslaved Israel in this land. The Lord came to Moses and reissued the promise of the land.

This land is a major theme in the Book of Deuteronomy. Moses repeatedly tells Israel that the land is a gift, flowing from God's grace. It is a place not just of "milk and honey" (Exodus 3:8; Leviticus 20:24; Numbers 13:27), but an abundant expanse in every way. It has "hills and valleys" through which rivers run (Deuteronomy 11:11). The Lord loves this land. His eyes are always on it.

The Land of Promise

At first glance, it does not appear that the New Testament is concerned about the Promised Land. What was so important to Israel looks to be nearly absent in the New Testament. However, a closer look shows that Israel's land promises had a tremendous impact on the Church. Consider the following parallels.

The land is a down payment. Abraham wanted to bury Sarah in the Promised Land, so he bought a cave at Machpelah from Ephron the Hittite (Genesis 23). This was the only plot of ground the patriarchs possessed. Still, they clung to God's promise: "To your offspring I give this land, from the river of Egypt to the great river, the river Euphrates" (Genesis 15:18). Abraham, Isaac, and Jacob lived by faith, not by sight. They were sojourners or resident aliens. They never possessed the land.

Christians are likewise "strangers" and "aliens" (1 Peter 1:1; 2:11 NIV), while we also have a down payment in the gift of the Holy Spirit. Like the patriarchs, we have a foretaste of the future, and this imparts much joy as we anticipate the full gift of our heavenly promised land.

The land is an inheritance. God repeatedly promises Israel that He will give Israel the land. After Joshua defeats enemy nations and parcels out the land, he tells the people, "You know in your hearts and souls, all of you, that not one word has failed of all the good things that the Lord your God promised concerning you. All have come to pass for you; not one of them has failed" (Joshua 23:14). Israel finally had the land, often called an "inheritance" (e.g., Leviticus 20:24; Numbers 26:53–56). And though individuals could lose their land, it was to be returned in the Year of Jubilee. Land was a lasting inheritance.

Baptized into Christ, we also have a permanent inheritance. Because of the resurrection of Jesus, we have an inheritance that can never perish, spoil, or fade. God vigilantly guards it in heaven for us.

Living in the land is the abundant life. Israel's land is "an exceedingly good land" (Numbers 14:7). It is "a land of brooks of water, of fountains and springs, flowing out in the valleys and hills, a land of wheat and barley, of vines and fig trees and pomegranates, a land of olive trees and honey" (Deuteronomy 8:7–8). Moses announces, "And the Lord will make you abound in prosperity, in the fruit of your womb and in the fruit of your livestock and in the fruit of your ground, within the land that the Lord swore to your fathers to give you" (Deuteronomy 28:11). A certain sign that Israel was under God's judgment was their exile *from the land*. To be "in the land," then, was to be where God funneled His gifts.

Being "in Christ" is to be where God graciously imparts His benefits of forgiveness, life, and salvation. Paul reminds us that we have been blessed "with every spiritual blessing in the heavenly places" (Ephesians 1:3). Our Savior says that life with Him is an abundant life (see John 10:10). Outside of Christ, there is only darkness and weeping and gnashing of teeth.

The land is a place of rest. The Lord promises that when Israel enters the land, He will give "rest from all your enemies around, so that you live in safety" (Deuteronomy 12:10). After Moses' death, Joshua recalls his words: "The Lord your God is providing you a place of rest and will give you this land" (Joshua 1:13).

For us, this promise comports with an idea expressed in the Book of Hebrews. Christians have the land (described as the rest into which we have entered through Christ) in a way even Joshua did not achieve for Israel. Jesus promises, "Come to Me, all who labor and are heavy laden, and I will give you rest" (Matthew 11:28). Those who die in faith enter their final rest. "'Blessed indeed,' says the Spirit, 'that they may rest from their labors, for their deeds follow them!'" (Revelation 14:13).

The land is a missional strategy. God's gift of the land to Abraham and his descendants was strategic. Two major trade routes, the Way of the Sea and the King's Highway, ran through the Promised Land and connected it with the cradles of civilization, Egypt and Mesopotamia. God's goal was for the nations to come into contact with Israel and, through Israel, to encounter His love and mercy—as Israel lived faithful to the covenant, "for that will be your wisdom and your understanding in the sight of the peoples, who, when they hear all these statutes, will say, 'Surely this great nation is a wise and understanding people.' For what great nation is there that has a god so near to it as the LORD our God is to us, whenever we call upon Him?" (Deuteronomy 4:6–7).

In a similar manner, the Church is empowered to be "a city set on a hill that cannot be hidden" (Matthew 5:14), so that our light shines before the nations and we praise our Father who is in heaven.

The Promise Fulfilled

God's promises to us can be confusing. Sometimes, we just cannot see how they could ever come to pass. God's ways are indeed confounding. For instance, we can recall that to bear His promised children, the Lord chooses barren women—Sarah, Rebekah, and Rachel. Who could have ever imagined such a thing! It was certainly not what anyone would have expected.

And who gets the Promised Land? Do the high and mighty? No. "The meek will inherit the land and enjoy great peace" (Psalm 37:11 NIV). The Promised Land is given to patriarchs who are marginalized Arameans. Later, it is given to Babylonian exiles who are likewise forlorn and hopeless. In Christ, God continues to choose what is "low and despised" (1 Corinthians 1:28). He selects the meek to inherit the earth. This pledge will be fulfilled when Christ comes again to give believers "new heavens and a new earth in which righteousness dwells" (2 Peter 3:13). Then He will welcome us, saying, "Go to the land I will show you!"

Whose Land Is It?

ASSYRIANS

Babylonians

Persians

GREEKS

ROMANS

Whose land is it, anyway? So many have owned it; so many have lived in it; so many have laid claim to it. To whom does it rightfully belong? Whose land is it? The Promised Land once belonged to the Amorites, and then it was possessed by the Israelites. Assyrians, Babylonians, Persians, Greeks, and Romans subsequently also claimed ownership. And since the end of the New Testament era, Byzantines, Ottomans, British, and Israelis have said they hold rights to the land. So whose land is it?

Some Popular Notions

From the fall of Jerusalem in AD 70 until the nineteenth century, the question of who owned Palestine was answered politically. Whoever had enough military muscle controlled the Promised Land. In the 1840s, however, a Plymouth Brethren minister from England named John Nelson Darby began teaching that the question of Palestine's ownership needed to be answered theologically. By introducing the method of biblical interpretation called dispensational premillennialism, Darby heralded the idea that biblical history is divided into seven "dispensations," or periods of time. The end of the sixth dispensation, he maintained, will be triggered by the Jewish return to their ancestral land.

Picking up where Darby left off, Cyrus Scofield propagated dispensational premillennialism in his influential *Scofield Reference Bible*, first published in 1909. That book is the single most important document espousing the teaching that God gave the land of Palestine to the Jews forever. Prior to these teachings of Darby and Scofield, most Christians (including Lutherans) understood the ownership of Palestine to be a political issue, not a theological one. All of that has changed. There are now millions of Christians who embrace the idea that the 1948 state of Israel is by divine decree and a sign that we are living in the last days. At any moment, they say, Christians are going to be raptured, and then the world will undergo a hell-like seven-year tribulation. At the end of these seven years, Christ will return, defeat the antichrist, and commence the seventh dispensation, His thousand-year reign on earth. Is this true?

When Jesus speaks about the land (Luke 19:41–44), He makes no reference to it ever being restored to the Jews. Nor does He sympathize with the Emmaus disciples and their hope for a redemption of Israel, which meant the end of Roman occupation and freedom for Jews to govern their own land. Christ's kingdom is not of this world, so He rebukes His traveling companions on the road to Emmaus for their dullness and slowness to understand the Old Testament prophets who wrote about Him (Luke 24:25–27). Jesus then teaches that everything in the Old Testament points to Him, not to the nationalistic hopes of first-century Jews. His disciples are not to anticipate a Jewish return to the Promised Land, but to look for the coming of the Son of Man in His glory on the Last Day.

In spite of these clear directives, the disciples shared the same nationalistic understanding of the land as the other Jews of the first century. Even *after* Christ's resurrection, they ask Him, "Lord, will You at this time restore the kingdom to Israel?" (Acts 1:6). After the coming of the Holy Spirit on the Day of Pentecost, the Church began to use Old Testament language concerning the land in new ways. In Romans 4:13, for example, Paul does not offer the promise of "land" to Abraham's offspring, but instead indicates that baptized believers will inherit "the world." By this, he maintains that God promises Christians a new heaven and a new earth. The question, then, is not whether the land promises of the Old Testament are to be understood literally or spiritually. Instead, the question is whether they should be interpreted in terms of Old Testament shadows or in terms of New Testament realities.

There is no suggestion that Jesus or His apostles ever believed the Jewish people had a divine right to the land or that the Jewish possession of the land would be an important, let alone central, aspect of God's plan for the world. Nor does the New Testament teach that the creation of an Israeli state will inaugurate the last days just before the rapture of the Church.

All of this is tied to the question "Whose land is it?" Canaan was promised to Abraham, taken possession of under Joshua, lost in the Assyrian (721 BC) and Babylonian (587 BC) exiles, regained by Judah upon Cyrus's decree (538 BC), and subsequently reinterpreted by New Testament authors. Paul, for his part, teaches that the land promises God gave to Abraham are made effective through Christ, Abraham's true Seed. All spiritual benefits are derived from Jesus, and apart from Him there is no participation in the promises made to Abraham. These are not directed toward any particular ethnic group. Nor do they concern the land of Palestine. The Church is the true Israel of God, and the baptized are the children of Abraham. We anticipate our full land inheritance when Christ comes again to give us the heavenly promised land.

When dispensational premillennialists point to the 1948 state of Israel as a concrete manifestation of God's presence, they overlook the fact that God *has* left visible and tangible signs indicating that He is with His people. "For there are three that testify: the Spirit, the water and the blood; and these three agree" (1 John 5:7–8). The Father testifies to being present with His Church right now by means of the Spirit-inspired and Christ-centered Old and New Testament Scriptures, the water of Baptism, as well as the true body and blood of Jesus in Holy Communion. The assurance of God's working in the world is not based on the return of the Jews to their ancestral land, but rather on the sure Word of promise of forgiveness of sins imparted in the Means of Grace—the Gospel and the Sacraments.

Reality Revealed

The promises God has made to us in the Scriptures can, at times, seem rather confusing. This is especially true of the Old Testament books of the Bible. The Old Testament can seem obscure and foreign. All the references to the people of Israel and the land of Canaan can be confusing. It can be tempting to read the newspaper and try to match current events of the Middle East with the promises of God.

Our hope is not based on current events in the Middle East and the Israeli occupation of the land. Rather, we fix our eyes on Jesus, even as we long and pray for his second and final advent. On that day, He will raise us from the dead and usher us into the new heavens and the new earth.

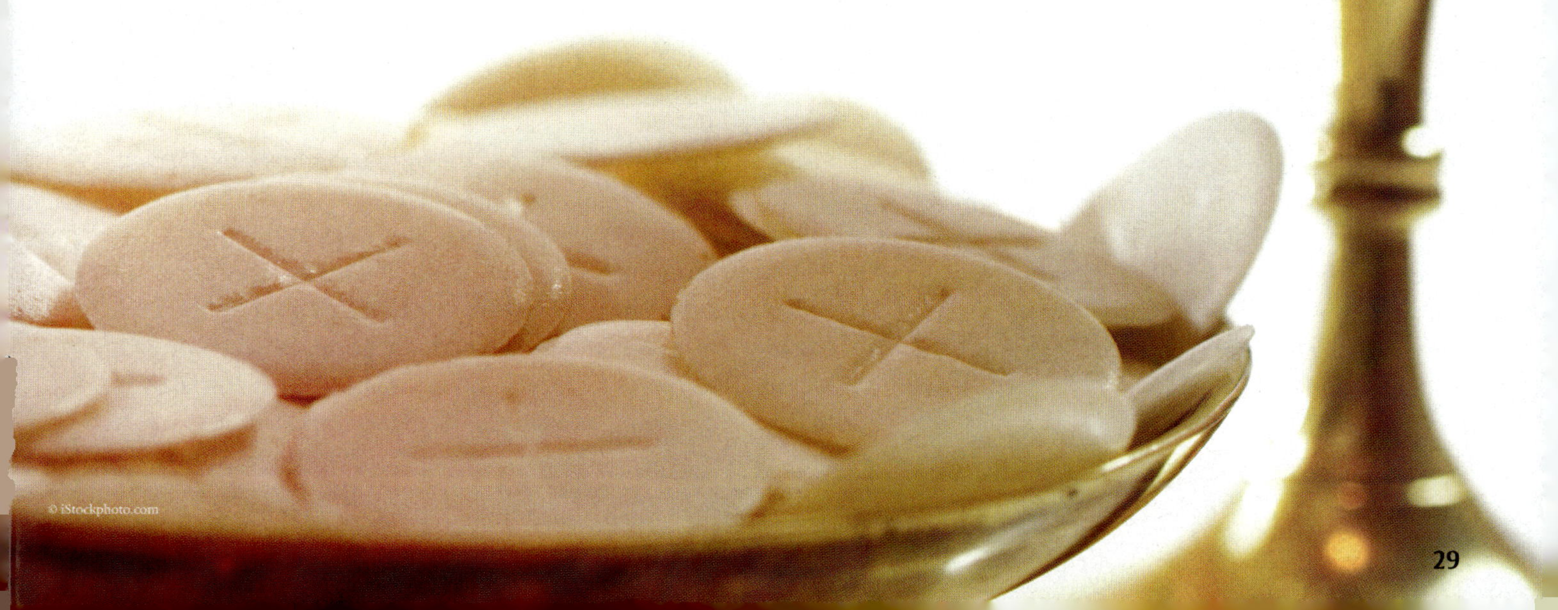

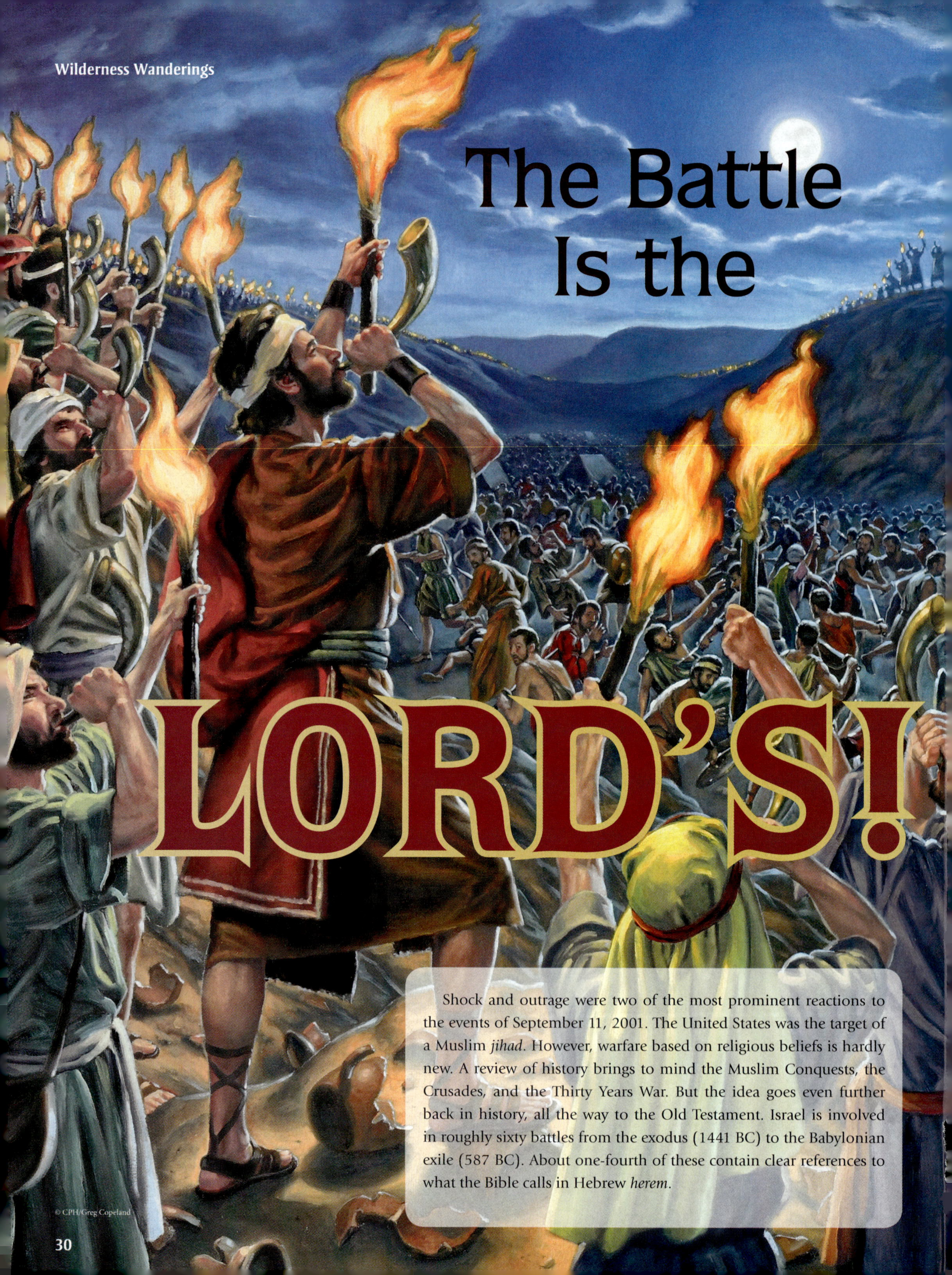

© CPH/Greg Copeland

The Battle Is the LORD'S!

Shock and outrage were two of the most prominent reactions to the events of September 11, 2001. The United States was the target of a Muslim *jihad*. However, warfare based on religious beliefs is hardly new. A review of history brings to mind the Muslim Conquests, the Crusades, and the Thirty Years War. But the idea goes even further back in history, all the way to the Old Testament. Israel is involved in roughly sixty battles from the exodus (1441 BC) to the Babylonian exile (587 BC). About one-fourth of these contain clear references to what the Bible calls in Hebrew *herem*.

Holy War

The term *herem* is difficult to translate. It may be rendered "banned" or "devoted things" and refers to plundered items and people captured during the course of a holy war. Moses commands the people, "And when the Lord your God gives them [Israel's enemies] over to you, and you defeat them, then you must devote them to complete destruction [*herem*]. You shall make no covenant with them and show no mercy to them" (Deuteronomy 7:2). This is hardly an isolated idea. Moses reiterates, "Know therefore today that He who goes over before you as a consuming fire is the Lord your God. He will destroy them and subdue them before you. So you shall drive them out and make them perish quickly, as the Lord has promised you" (Deuteronomy 9:3). Following these commands was an act of worship.

"Show no mercy to them"? (Deuteronomy 7:2). What are we to make of this? It doesn't sound Christian at all! How do these texts relate to New Testament admonitions such as love your enemies, turn the other cheek, walk the extra mile, and "bless and do not curse" (Romans 12:14)? If genocide and ethnic cleansing are morally wrong in the twenty-first century, weren't they also wrong in the fifteenth or thirteenth centuries BC? How are the atrocities of our day that are done in the name of religion different from the slaughter of Canaanite men, women, and children prisoners of war that we read about in the Old Testament?

Herem presents a moral dilemma for Christian readers of the Old Testament. How should we understand the command to annihilate our enemy? One way people approach this problem is to discard these parts of the Old Testament because Israel's Great Commission appears to be one of destruction as opposed to the New Testament's mission of love, forgiveness, and reconciliation. The idea is that *herem* texts in the Old Testament document Israel's history but have no authoritative voice for the Church. Holy war texts of the Old Testament are therefore pre-Christ, sub-Christ, and anti-Christ.

The critique of this view is that—if not in theory, then in practice—it decanonizes major sections of the Old Testament. If we marginalize holy war texts, then we can no longer affirm with Paul that all of Israel's Scriptures are "profitable for teaching, for reproof, for correction, and for training in righteousness" (2 Timothy 3:16). What is more, the position that drives a wedge between the testaments overlooks this fact. "The Lord is a man of war" (Exodus 15:3), but so is Jesus. He "judges and makes war," is "clothed in a robe dipped in blood," and out of His mouth "comes a sharp sword with which to strike down the nations" (Revelation 19:11–15). At times, the Savior also calls down curses on His enemies, as did Paul.

Spiritual War

Yes, there is a certain amount of discontinuity between the *herem* texts in the Old Testament and our life in Christ. We are never called on to resort to physical violence. And yet we are in a battle, though not with "flesh and blood." Rather, our fight is "against the rulers, against the authorities, against the cosmic powers over this present darkness" (Ephesians 6:12).

Israel's battles were also against spiritual enemies. The Song of Moses not only celebrates the Lord's triumph over Pharaoh and his armies but also has clear overtones of an even more profound and significant victory, one over every counterfeit god. "Who is like You, O Lord, among the gods? Who is like You, majestic in holiness, awesome in glorious deeds, doing wonders?" (Exodus 15:11). The judgment on Pharaoh and Egypt was a judgment on their gods. Deborah's song indicates that God's battles take place on two levels—one on earth and the other in heaven (Judges 5:19–20). There is continuity between Israel's warfare and the Church's because both fight "against the spiritual forces of evil in the heavenly places" (Ephesians 6:12).

We share Israel's battle strategy. Giving a war shout of joy before battle appears to be strategic in several Israelite military assaults. For example, in Joshua 6, the priests blow trumpets for six days as they process around Jericho with the ark of the covenant. On the seventh day, they march around the city seven times. Joshua then commands the people, "Shout, for the Lord has given you the city" (Joshua 6:16). Also instructive are the events in 2 Chronicles 20. In this chapter, the Lord gains a victory over the Ammonites, Edomites, and Moabites. But how does He do it? First, a Levitical singer named Jahaziel son of Zechariah prophesies triumph. Next, some Levites from the Kohathites and Korahites stand up and sing praises to God. Then the climactic words of 2 Chronicles 20:21: "[Jehoshaphat] appointed those who were to sing to the Lord and praise Him in holy attire, as they went before the army, and say, 'Give thanks to the Lord, for His steadfast love endures forever.'" With this battle cry, the enemies were thrown into confusion and easily defeated.

© Val Lawless/iStockphoto.com

The Sure and Certain Victory

At times, it may well be a disturbing thought for us; nevertheless, it is true. We do have enemies who try to assault us spiritually so that we would come to despair of God's mercy. The world, the devil, and our own sinful flesh all work against us, attempting to smother the faith in Christ within us.

Although we find ourselves engaged in this conflict, it is not something that should cause us to fear. In fact, we are invited to enter into battle against our spiritual enemies with songs and praises, confident that God in Jesus Christ has equipped us for victory. Confronted with injustice, Paul and Silas sing hymns to God. And when the churches in Asia Minor experience great anguish, John does not instruct them to take up arms. Rather, he gives them a victory shout: "Worthy is the Lamb who was slain, to receive power and wealth and wisdom and might and honor and glory and blessing!" (Revelation 5:12). This is our way of saying, "The battle is the Lord's" (1 Samuel 17:47).

© Christopher Futcher/iStockphoto.com